Dundee CHANGIN

D1470703

CARAE UXORI MEAE

Law Essentials

ROMAN LAW

Craig Anderson, LL.B.

Lecturer in Law,
Robert Gordon University, Aberdeen

DUNDEE UNIVERSITY PRESS
2009

First edition published in Great Britain in 2009 by
Dundee University Press
University of Dundee
Dundee DD1 4HN

www.dup.dundee.ac.uk

ISBN 978 1 84586 084 4

No natural forests were destroyed to make this product;
only farmed timber was used and replanted.

British Library Cataloguing-in-Publication Data
A catalogue record for this book is available on request from the British Library

Typeset by Waverley Typesetters, Fakenham
Printed and bound by Bell & Bain Ltd, Glasgow

CONTENTS

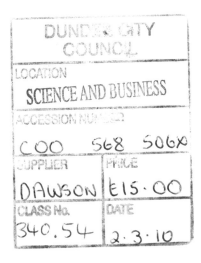

TABLE OF CASES

TABLE OF STATUTES

NOTE ON THE CITATION OF ROMAN SOURCES

In this book, and other books on Roman law, reference is made to Roman sources. It is therefore important to know how to find and how to cite these.

The main source of our knowledge of Roman law is the *Digest* of Justinian. The *Digest* is divided into a number of books, and each book into a number of titles, each with a number. Each title is further subdivided. A passage in the *Digest* is cited with the abbreviation "D", followed by the number of the book, then the number of the title, and so on. Thus, the first title of the first book is cited as D.1.1.

Each title is divided into *leges* (laws), each of which is an extract from a particular author. The name of the author and the work from which it is taken are given at the beginning. The *leges* themselves are numbered.

Each *lex* is further subdivided into paragraphs. The first is cited by adding "pr" (for *principium*, or beginning) to the citation for the section. Thus, the opening words of the *Digest* would be cited as D.1.1.1pr. Thereafter, each paragraph is numbered, so the next is D.1.1.1.1.

The other Roman sources are cited in much the same way, but with different letters at the beginning. Passages in the *Institutes* of Justinian are cited with the letter "J" (or sometimes "Inst"), passages in the *Codex* of Justinian with "C" and passages in the *Novels* with the abbreviation "Nov". Citations beginning "G" relate to the *Institutes* of Gaius.

1 HISTORICAL INTRODUCTION

On entering law school, the beginning student will often be presented with a timetable that includes the study of Roman law. For many others, Roman law will be an optional subject in their degree programme. It would not be unreasonable for such a student to be surprised by this, and to ask why the law of ancient Rome should be thought relevant to the study of 21st-century law.

One answer to this question lies in the general historical importance of Rome in European history. The dominant position of Rome and her empire for so many centuries certainly justifies the attention of anyone who considers history important. The law of Rome, as perhaps the most outstanding product of that civilisation, deserves a special place in any account of the history of Rome. The process of development of a sophisticated system of law was much more advanced among the Romans than anywhere else in the ancient world. The beginner may well be surprised by how much like modern legal texts the Roman texts look. For this reason, even in countries where the direct influence of Roman law has been limited, the study of Roman law is seen as valuable in developing legal thinking in students.

Of more immediate relevance to the modern law student, though, is the fact that the private law of Rome is not a matter of purely historical interest. Unlike any other ancient system of law, Roman law survived into later history and came to form the basis of many modern systems. Thus, for Scots law, it may be said that in many areas the influence of Roman law is so great that they cannot be fully understood without a proper understanding of their Roman basis. This may even understate the case somewhat, for Roman law is still a living source of law in Scotland today, with Roman authorities not infrequently being cited before the Scottish courts. The importance of knowledge of Roman law to the Scots lawyer is such that it is a prerequisite for admission to the Faculty of Advocates.

The purpose of this book is to give an introductory overview of the main institutions of Roman private law, together with an outline of its later history. For the most part, public law is not covered, as by far the greater part of the Roman influence on later law was in respect of private law. However, Roman law cannot be fully understood without an understanding of the historical context in which it developed. For this reason, the remainder of this chapter is devoted to an outline of the history of Rome.

PERIODS OF ROMAN HISTORY

Roman history is traditionally divided into a number of distinct periods, based on the changing structure of Rome's government.

The first period – the Monarchy – begins with the traditional foundation date of Rome in 753 BC, and lasts until the expulsion of the last king in 510 BC.

The second period is the Republic. For almost five centuries following 510 BC, Rome was governed according to a republican constitution.

The third and final period – the Empire – began in 27 BC. From this year, the governance of Rome and its empire lay ultimately in the hands of one man, the emperor, who was in substance a monarch, though not named as such. Through time, the nature of the emperor's role as being in effect that of a monarch became more explicit. Accordingly, the Empire is further subdivided into two periods. In the earlier period (the Principate), the Republican constitution was preserved relatively intact, though subject to the ultimate authority of the emperor. In the later period (the Dominate), the importance of the Republican institutions had declined to the point where the emperor could be openly seen as *dominus*, or master, of the Roman world. The Dominate is dated from the accession of the emperor Diocletian in AD 284, and lasted in the western part of the Empire until its fall in AD 476. The Eastern Empire survived until the fall of its capital, Constantinople, to the Ottomans in 1453.

THE ORIGINS OF ROME AND THE ROMANS

Little reliable evidence is available for early Roman history, and no detailed written account survives from before the 3rd century BC – centuries after the events in question.

For the Romans, their existence as a people began with the legendary Trojan hero Aeneas, who, with his followers, fled the fall of Troy to the Greeks. Aeneas had various adventures, recounted by the Roman poet Virgil in the *Aeneid*, including a torrid love affair with Dido, the Queen of Carthage in North Africa. Abandoning Dido, who then committed suicide swearing eternal enmity between Carthage and Aeneas's people, Aeneas and his followers proceeded north and settled in Italy, near the mouth of the Tiber.

Rome itself was held to have been founded in 753 BC by twin brothers: Romulus and Remus. The city was named after Romulus, who became its first king after murdering Remus in a dispute over an omen.

Early Rome was an agricultural community much like any other in the region, Latium (modern Lazio). There was nothing at this stage to indicate its future greatness, although it was situated at an important crossing point of the Tiber, which perhaps was what brought Rome under the influence of the Etruscans, an advanced and sophisticated civilisation to the north, in Etruria (modern Tuscany). Indeed, it has been suggested that Rome was founded by the Etruscans. However that may be, though, Rome was influenced from an early stage by the Etruscans, in whose shadow Rome initially developed, and at least two of Rome's last three kings were probably Etruscans.

THE MONARCHY

As we have seen, early Rome was a monarchy. The available evidence does not allow us to say with certainty what were the kings' precise functions and powers, but the monarchy was certainly elective in nature, each of the supposedly six successors to Romulus being confirmed in office by a citizen assembly established by him and called the *comitia curiata*.

Information about individual kings is also limited. We do not even know how many there were. The traditional number, seven, comes to us from king lists written down at a later date, but some scepticism may be justified by the fact that the seven kings over the 243 years of the Monarchy would have an average reign of almost 35 years, in an age when life expectancy would have been much lower than it is today.

Patricians and plebeians

During the reign of Romulus, an advisory council, called the Senate, was established. From this came the division of Roman society into two classes, or Orders. The descendants of the members of the Senate were called patricians, and the rest of the population were called plebeians and were subject to various legal and social restrictions.

The development of Rome

We have seen that early Rome was an agricultural community. However, during the Monarchy it began to develop. Particularly during the reigns of the later kings, there were extensive public works, transforming Rome into a city with paved streets, walls and drainage.

Externally, too, Rome was developing. It was gradually acquiring territory and influence. By the end of the Monarchy, through a combination of diplomacy and armed force, Rome controlled perhaps between

300 and 400 square miles. This, of course, is trifling compared with the extent of the Roman Empire at its height. Indeed, it is less than the urban area of the modern city of Rome. However, it was enough at this time to make Rome the dominant city in Latium. More was to come.

THE REPUBLIC

In 510 BC, the monarchy was abolished and Rome became a Republic. The last king, Tarquinius Superbus, was said to have been a tyrant. However, according to tradition, the immediate cause of his overthrow was the rape by his son of Lucretia, the wife of a Roman noble, and Lucretia's subsequent suicide. The fact, though, that this led to an overthrow of the monarchy itself rather than just the overthrow of an individual monarch perhaps suggests disenchantment with monarchical government.

Certainly, throughout the Republic there seemed to be a fear of having ultimate power concentrated in the hands of one man. The powers of the kings were transferred, not to a single ruler, but to joint rulers. At the head of the Republican constitution stood two annually elected magistrates known as consuls, each of whom had a veto over the other. In emergencies, a single ruler, called a *dictator*, could be appointed, but with a restricted term of office of 6 months.

The Republican constitution

The Roman fear of tyranny permeated the Republican constitution. Even where the consuls were able to work together (which could by no means be guaranteed), their power was restricted by the existence of other magistrates exercising their own jurisdiction. Legislation was the responsibility of the citizen assemblies, and the consuls' power would also be limited by political considerations.

Of the other magistrates, the most important from the lawyers' point of view were the praetors. These magistrates were first appointed from 367 BC with responsibility over the civil law. The urban praetor had jurisdiction over disputes involving Roman citizens, and another praetor, known as the peregrine praetor, had jurisdiction over disputes involving foreigners (*peregrini*). We shall see more about the praetors' functions in Chapters 2 and 10.

Of the remaining magistrates, the aediles had various duties relating to the care of the city and its inhabitants, such as the maintenance of supplies of food and water and of public roads and buildings.

The quaestors were magistrates with responsibility in financial matters, and also a role in the consuls' criminal jurisdiction. From 494 BC, plebeian magistrates called tribunes were elected to represent plebeian interests. The tribunes had the right to veto any act by another magistrate, and presided over *concilium plebis*, an assembly made up of plebeian citizens, which became during the Republic the main legislative organ. From 443 BC, responsibility for the compilation of the census was given to the censors. They were appointed for periods of up to 18 months, and classified citizens for military, political and taxation purposes. The office of censor involved supervision of the morals of the people, with the right to place a mark of disgrace against a person's name, with various social and legal consequences. The censors also acquired the responsibility for appointment of senators, though in practice this was restricted to the power to exclude a man from the Senate.

In addition to these magistracies, there were also citizen assemblies, which alone had the power to legislate. However, the assemblies had no legislative initiative, and could meet only when summoned by the appropriate magistrate. In practice, the dominant political institution in the Republic was the Senate. All of the magistracies (except the censorship) lasting only a year, the Senate was the stable part of the Republican constitution, and, as the Senate was made up of the leading men of the state, mostly former magistrates, it would be a rare magistrate who disregarded it.

The Struggle of the Orders

We have seen that Roman citizenry was divided into two parts: patricians and plebeians. Unsurprisingly, there was plebeian discontent at a status which was in many ways inferior. The magistracies were restricted to patricians, for example, and the plebeian assembly had an inferior status. This discontent led to pressure for reform, on occasion involving threats by the plebeians to secede and found a new city. This is known as the Struggle of the Orders. As a result of this, gradual concessions were made. One of these, the establishment of the office of tribune, as a magistrate representing the plebeians, we have already seen. From 367 BC, too, one of the two consuls was required to be a plebeian. In 287 BC, legislation of the plebeian assembly was made fully binding on the whole citizen body.

From the point of view of the study of Roman law, the most important development was the publication of the law in 451–450 BC in the Twelve Tables. The Twelve Tables are considered in Chapter 2.

Roman expansion

Throughout the Republic, Rome was frequently involved in conflict. Within 15 years of the establishment of the Republic, Rome had defeated the Etruscans in alliance with other Latin states, and then defeated the Latin states. By the early 3rd century BC, Rome had secured its position as the dominant power in central Italy. This century then saw Rome become dominant over the whole of Italy, following defeats of the Gallic tribes of the north of the Italian peninsula and of the Greek city states of the south.

It should not be thought, however, that success was purely a result of military conquest. First, Rome was at this period generally willing to extend the hand of friendship to defeated enemies, who would often become allies, with Rome the dominant partner. Second, the foundation of colonies helped secure conquered territories. A third factor in Rome's success was the development of a network of roads with Rome at its centre. Nor should it be thought that conquest was necessarily Rome's primary aim. Much of Rome's rise to dominance in Italy was a result of dealing with specific problems as they arose, without there being necessarily a grand plan of conquest.

As Rome expanded, however, it became less generous to its allies. Demands for Roman citizenship to be extended to Rome's Italian allies led to the allies to revolt against Rome in 91 BC. Although in purely military terms Rome won the Social War, as this war is known (from *socii*, meaning "allies"), to gain that victory it was compelled to concede Roman citizenship to those Italians who would lay down their arms.

Rome's rise to prominence inevitably brought it into conflict with other powers. During this period, the dominant power in the western Mediterranean was Carthage. Rome fought three wars with Carthage: from 264 BC to 261 BC over control of Sicily; from 218 BC to 201 BC over control of Spain; and in 146 BC. In the first two of these wars, Rome was stretched to the limit, but won. The third war destroyed Carthaginian power, and indeed Carthage itself, for the city was destroyed and its inhabitants sold into slavery. This left Rome dominant in the western Mediterranean.

In the eastern Mediterranean, advantage was taken of the disintegration of Alexander the Great's empire following his death in 323 BC. Through a combination of diplomacy and military force, by the 1st century BC Rome controlled much of the eastern Mediterranean.

Rome also expanded to the north, and in the 2nd century BC created a new province in southern Gaul (modern France), in part to protect the land route to Spain. The conquest of Gaul was completed by Julius Caesar in 52 BC, following a lengthy campaign.

THE FALL OF THE REPUBLIC

The Republican constitution was not stable. The system of consuls was designed for the specific situation of avoiding a return to the tyranny of rule by monarchs, and it was designed for a small state, not for an empire. The expansion of Rome exacerbated the problems inherent in joint rule by potential rivals.

In the last century or so before the establishment of the Empire, the Republican constitution came increasingly under threat. By this time, the Roman army was a professional force dependent, for its pay and conditions, on its generals. Several generals were able to use this fact to enforce their will and seize power. The most important of these was Julius Caesar.

Following his conquest of Gaul, Caesar returned to Italy. Ignoring a decree requiring him to resume his status as a private citizen, Caesar crossed the Rubicon, the river marking the boundary of Italy, with his army in 49 BC. In the civil war that followed, Caesar emerged victorious and was appointed dictator for life. Although he publicly refused to be crowned king, this was too open an attempt to grab personal power, and Caesar was assassinated in 44 BC.

Caesar's assassination did not, however, lead to the restoration of the Republic for which his killers hoped. Factional fighting and further civil war led in 27 BC to the emergence of Caesar's heir, Octavian (later Augustus) as *de facto* emperor.

THE PRINCIPATE

Augustus learned from the mistakes of the past. There was to be no open break with the past, and no open grab for personal power. Augustus gradually acquired monarchical powers, and was in effect monarch, but was careful to do this so far as possible within the Republican constitution. Thus, he avoided terms such as "king" or "dictator", and was instead known by the title of "*princeps*", which might be translated as "first citizen". In this way, Augustus could claim to be protecting the Republic rather than destroying it.

In form, the new government was a partnership between Augustus and the Senate but, as time went on, it was increasingly Augustus and his successors who were the dominant partners. The Senate and the

Assemblies continued to exist, magistrates continued to be elected, but always subject to the ultimate authority of the emperor. The Senate retained its prestige perhaps longer than the other institutions, but all of these became in the end mouthpieces of the emperor.

THE DOMINATE

By the 3rd century AD, there was a new period of crisis. The Roman Empire had by now grown to extend from Britain to the Middle East. It was too big to be ruled by one single, central authority. The emperors were dependent on the army for their power, and permanently ran the risk of being usurped by some general who had been declared emperor by his own troops. Military incursions by external forces led to increases in taxation at the same time as they reduced the ability of the people to pay, with resulting economic problems. It is hardly surprising that 18 emperors reigned during the period AD 235–284.

Diocletian was declared emperor by army in AD 284, which was by now the traditional way. He realised the need to reform the government of the Empire. In his reign, the Empire was divided into east and west, each with its own emperor. Diocletian, the supreme emperor, took the eastern part, symptomatic of a general shift eastwards in the Empire's centre of gravity. Each emperor had a junior partner, designated heir. In addition, Diocletian worked to reduce the political influence of the army. He also promoted the idea of the emperor as monarch. From now on, the emperor was to be *dominus* (master), rather than *princeps*.

Two particular emperors reigning during the Dominate call for special attention: Constantine and Justinian, the former reigning before the fall of the Western Empire, and the latter reigning afterwards.

Constantine

Following Diocletian's abdication in AD 305, Constantine emerged as sole emperor following a civil war. His reign is notable mainly for two major developments.

The first of these is the toleration of Christianity, and Constantine's subsequent conversion to Christianity. In the earlier centuries AD, Christians had been persecuted, but all of Constantine's successors but one were Christians.

The second development was the foundation of a new capital at Constantinople (the modern Istanbul). This was the culmination of the eastwards shift in power.

The fall of the Western Empire

Following the death of Theodosius I in AD 395, the Empire was split between his two sons, Arcadius and Honorius, abandoning Diocletian's system of a divided empire subject to one supreme emperor. To a great extent, the story is from here one of two empires, Eastern and Western, rather than one.

The Western Empire survived less than a century more. Overrun by incomers, there was a gradual retreat of Roman power. Rome itself was captured by the Visigoths in AD 410. Ultimately, the last emperor, Romulus Augustulus, was deposed in AD 476 by Germanic tribes under the leadership of Odoacer.

The Eastern Empire endured until the 15th century, though the latter part of that was a story of gradual retreat. However, there was some recovery under the reign of Justinian.

Justinian

Justinian I was born of a peasant family in Tauresium, modern-day Taor in the Republic of Macedonia. Unlike the majority in the Empire as it then stood, his native tongue was Latin rather than Greek. His uncle and adoptive father Justinus was proclaimed emperor in 518, having risen through the ranks of the army. Justinus died in 527, having made Justinian co-emperor earlier that year. From that point Justinian reigned as sole emperor.

From 527 until his death in 565, Justinian reigned with vigour and skill. One of his major interests was in religion, and he took an active role in the religious disputes of his day. He was also responsible for the building of the Church of the Holy Wisdom in Constantinople.

As far as secular politics was concerned, Justinian's goal was nothing less than the restoration of the glory of the Empire at its height. In this, he benefited from an ability to pick talented men to carry out his aims. Under the leadership of his generals, Narses and Belisarius, Roman armies once again marched forward to conquest. Much territory that had been lost was regained during Justinian's rule. Italy, including Rome itself, was brought back within the Empire. However, these gains proved fragile, most of Italy being lost again within 3 years of Justinian's death.

More important for our purposes was the collection of Roman law made under Justinian's direction, the *Corpus Iuris Civilis*. This task was delegated to another talented underling, Tribonian, a senior officer of state. It is through this collection that almost all of our knowledge of Roman law comes. It is considered further in Chapter 2.

Essential Facts

- Roman private law forms the basis of many modern legal systems, including much of Scots law.
- Roman history is divided into several distinct periods. The early period, the Monarchy, when Rome was subject to the rule of kings, traditionally lasted from 753 BC until the last king was deposed in 510 BC. The Republic lasted from then until Augustus became the first emperor in 27 BC. The Empire dates from this time, and is itself divided into two: the earlier period (the Principate) lasting until the accession of the emperor Diocletian in AD 284.
- Government in the Republic was divided among a number of magistrates, normally elected annually, who were advised by a council of prominent citizens called the Senate. The senior magistrates were the two consuls. Administration of private law was the responsibility of the praetors.
- Roman society was divided into two classes, or "Orders": the patricians and plebeians. During the Republic, the plebeians were gradually able to impose sufficient pressure to achieve concessions, culminating in political equality during the Republic.
- The fall of the Republic in 27 BC led to the establishment of a *de facto* monarchy. However, it was not until the Dominate that this could be proclaimed openly.
- The most important emperor in the Dominate from the legal point of view was Justinian. He was responsible for the great collection of Roman legal materials known as the *Corpus Iuris Civilis*.

2 SOURCES AND DEVELOPMENT OF ROMAN LAW

No system of law can remain static. The law develops through time. Roman law developed through various means. During the Monarchy, the main source was customary law, supplemented by royal decrees. With the demise of the Monarchy, other means of developing the law had to be found. This chapter looks at the three main sources of legal development: juristic interpretation; rules created by the urban praetor; and legislation. It finishes by looking at Justinian's great compilation of the law: the *Corpus Iuris Civilis* (itself enacted as legislation).

JURISTS

Part of the development of the law comes from its interpretation by experts. In the modern law, this is primarily the function of the courts. Some legal development also comes from interpretations of the law in the writings of legal scholars.

In the formative period of Roman law, as we shall see in Chapter 10, the courts were not presided over by legally trained judges. The courts could not therefore contribute to the development of the law in the way they do today. This role had to be taken by others.

In early Rome, the interpretation of the law fell within the remit of the priests. However, during the Republic a class of secular legal experts emerged, called jurists.

It should not be thought that the jurists were members of a legal profession in the modern sense. Rather, the jurists were men of the upper class, who took to the law as their contribution to public life. Nor can they have represented the whole body of teachers and advisers in the law. We know only of around 70 jurists by name, and as they constantly cited each others' works in their own writings it seems unlikely that there are many others whose names are lost to us. This number is hardly sufficient to deal with the legal business that would have arisen in Rome. There must, therefore, have been many lesser legal advisers who were not recognised as belonging to the elite inner circle of jurists.

An important respect in which the jurists differed from modern lawyers is that they did not generally represent parties in court. The actual conduct of litigation was carried out by advocates – men whose speciality was oratory rather than the law. There was some overlap, of course. Anyone acting as an advocate would doubtless pick up some of the law. The most famous advocate of them all, Cicero, was also knowledgeable in the law. Likewise, Quintus Mucius Scaevola, one of the leading jurists of the late Republic, also appeared in court as an advocate. However, by and large the distinction was maintained.

The jurists' role can be said to fall into three parts. First, they were legal advisers. The advised both private parties and public officials, such as the praetor. They might also advise a judge on a case that was before him. Secondly, they were writers. The jurists wrote large numbers of books of various types. It is through their writing that they are known to us. Thirdly, they taught students, usually through a type of apprenticeship rather than through formal classes.

As Republic gave way to Empire, this role continued. The classical period of Roman law continued through the Principate, and most of the surviving legal writings come from this period. However, as time wore on, the jurists increasingly became part of the Imperial administration, dealing with legal business on behalf of the emperor. As we shall see with the magistracies and Republican assemblies, in the Empire there was little room for legal innovation that was not under the control of the emperor. During the Dominate, lawyers for the most part are anonymous. The comparative lack of independent legal writing is part of the reason for the apparent decline in legal science in the Dominate, although it does seem that there was genuinely such a decline, with lawyers increasingly having difficulty working with the classical texts.

The juristic "schools"

Most or all jurists of the first two centuries AD belonged to one of two "schools": the Sabinian school and the Proculian school. These were founded by two jurists respectively called Capito and Labeo but they took their names from two of their subsequent heads, Sabinus and Proculus. Much is unclear about the nature and functioning of these schools, including the extent to which they were primarily schools of education or schools of thought.

Differences of opinion between these two schools appear throughout the surviving texts. On the whole, it can be said that the Proculians preferred an objective approach to the law, stressing rational argument from legal principles, while the Sabinians were readier to depart from adherence to principle when the facts justified it. It is not possible, however, to account for all of the differences between the two schools on such grounds.

Gaius and the Institutional Scheme

One of the legal writers whose name has come down to us is deserving of special comment. Gaius, who lived from around AD 110 until around AD 180, was writer of the *Institutes*, one of the most influential legal textbooks ever written. Until its rediscovery in 1816, the *Institutes* was thought to have survived only in the form of a later abridgement. However, it formed the basis of Justinian's *Institutes*, considered below, and is, as far as we know, the origin of the Institutional Scheme into which Roman law is traditionally structured.

The *Institutes* was written as an introductory textbook, and Gaius himself was probably a teacher. Certainly, he was not a member of the circle of leading jurists, and is not referred to by any other writer in the *Digest* (see below), although by the time of Justinian he had acquired sufficient prestige to be referred to as *Gaius noster* – "our own Gaius". He was also not a typical jurist in being interested in legal history and in systematisation of the law. Most jurists tended to take the approach of developing the law on a case-by-case basis. The importance of Gaius lies in his approach to the law.

Early law is a law of actions. This is certainly true for Roman law. The law consists of a number of specific claims, or actions, into one of which you must fit your facts. There might, for example, be an action to enforce a sale. However, as the law develops it becomes necessary to elaborate the requirements for each action. For example, who can bring the action? Against whom? On what facts? It comes to be realised that, underneath the procedure, there is a substantive right. Individual actions can be classified together as having some feature in common. For example, several actions will be based on a claim that there was some agreement between the parties. The Institutional Scheme involves separating the substance of the law from its procedures. In the example of a sale, the substance of the underlying agreement can be discussed together with other agreements as a "law of contracts", leaving purely procedural matters to be considered separately. The third part of the Institutional Scheme, the law of actions, is essentially what is left once the substantive legal rights that a person has are removed.

Gaius saw that rights could be divided into two types. Either they related to personal status, as with rights and obligations arising from marriage or parenthood, or they were what one might call "patrimonial rights". Gaius saw that rights arising from, say, a contract shared this characteristic with rights in the law of property, and so classed property and obligations together.

Gaius's great innovation, then, was in dividing the private law into three parts: the law of persons (ie the law relating to personal status) the law of things (ie property and obligations) and the law of actions (ie court procedures). Within each part of the tripartite division, the subject-matter was further subdivided. Thus, persons are first classified as either free persons or slaves. Free persons are classified as either free born or freed.

The Institutional Scheme is not perfect. There are several points on which the classification of a particular rule or institution can be criticised. Whatever else may be said, though, its success is clear in providing the law with a coherent framework. It provides a "map" of the law, allowing it to be readily seen how its different parts relate to each other. The influence of Gaius's scheme has been long lasting, and has been used or adapted by many into the modern period, even beyond introductory texts. For example, it is used as the basis for the definition of Scots private law in the Scotland Act 1998, s 126(4). According to that definition, Scots private law covers the "law of persons", the "law of obligations", the "law of property" and the "law of actions". Some writers have attempted to improve on the Institutional Scheme, but even when this is done it lies behind such innovations. The Scots institutional writers of the 17th and 18th centuries are examples of this.

The *ius respondendi*

We have seen that jurists had the function of developing the law through the giving of opinions. Such opinions were not, however, formally binding, and there was also the risk that there would be conflicting juristic opinion on a point in issue.

The jurist Pomponius tells us that Augustus conferred on some jurists the right to give legal opinions with the emperor's authority, the *ius respondendi*, which practice was continued by his successors. We are not, however, told the nature of this authority or how many jurists had it. It would be inconsistent with the general approach taken by Augustus to make an open break with the past, so it may be that the purpose was only to mark out particular jurists with imperial favour, rather than to make the jurist's opinion formally binding. Of course, in practice it would be a rare judge who would refuse to follow the opinion of a jurist who had been marked out with imperial favour.

The Law of Citations

We have seen that much of the sophistication of the classical law was a result of juristic debate. Jurists would in their writings refer to others' opinions, whether to disagree or to add weight to their own views. This process, however, led to the production of vast quantities of legal writing. The lawyers of the Dominate found it difficult to work with the volume of literature that had come to them from the classical jurists. This doubtless contributed to the popularity of Gaius's systematic exposition of the law in the *Institutes*.

To deal with this difficulty, the Law of Citations was introduced in AD 426 by the emperor Theodosius II. The Law of Citations named five classical jurists (Gaius, Papinian, Paul, Ulpian and Modestinus) as having special authority. In the event of dispute, the majority opinion among those writers was to be followed, including in the count any quotation made in their works from another jurist. If numbers among those expressing a view were even, Papinian was to be followed. Only failing those rules was the judge entitled to make up his own mind. The rules established by the Law of Citations have been criticised as mechanical, but in an age of decline in legal science they at least have the merit of practical expediency. In any case, the extent to which this was a mechanical process can be overestimated. It may be noted at this point that the Law of Citations is not very different from the modern rules of precedent, which equally require courts to follow prior decisions on a basis other than their merit.

THE PRAETOR

The praetor also had an important role in the development of Roman law, through his involvement in litigation. A fuller account of the role of the praetor will be found in Chapter 10. However, in brief, before taking a dispute before a judge, it was necessary to go first before the praetor to ask to be allowed an action. At this point, the appropriate form for the action would be decided.

The praetor's edict

As one of the higher magistrates, the praetor had the power to issue edicts, which were essentially statements of how they would discharge their responsibilities during their term of office. In the praetor's case, the edict he issued at the start of his term of office would state the circumstances in which he would allow an action. This edict would for the most part normally be taken over as it stood from the previous year's praetor. However, the praetor could and did innovate and add new actions.

The *ius honorarium*

Roman law was called "civil law", *ius civile*, as being the law of the Roman citizens, *cives*. Strictly, this law could be changed only by legislation. Although they controlled litigation, the praetors formally had no legislative competence. However, in practice, by controlling the giving of remedies the praetors controlled the development of the law. By creating a new action, the praetor was in effect creating new rights. Likewise, where the praetor qualified an existing remedy, he was qualifying a right that a party would otherwise have held. As the jurist Papinian put it, the praetors could introduce provisions in the edict "in the public interest ... in aid or supplementation or correction of the civil law" (D.1.1.7.1). Thus, the praetor might grant a defence to a civil law action, or allow a remedy not available under the civil law on the facts at issue. In theory, the civil law remained but in practice the praetor's edict was a source of substantive law reform. Such reforms usually appeared in the edict issued at the beginning of the praetor's term of office, but it was also possible, though much less usual, for a reform to be made during the praetor's term, if a party sought it and the praetor thought it appropriate. This law created by the praetor was named *ius honorarium* to distinguish it from the *ius civile*. As law, the praetor's edict itself attracted juristic consideration. Jurists were also responsible for much of the content of the edict. The praetor would not normally have legal expertise, and so would consult jurists on what he should include in the edict.

Changes in the Empire

In the Empire, it was not consistent with the new constitutional situation for anyone to be introducing legal reforms independently of the emperor. Thus, most of the legal developments coming through the *ius honorarium* came in the Republic. There was little such development in the Empire. As a result, the importance of the office of praetor declined. During the reign of Hadrian in the 2nd century AD, the jurist Julian was commissioned to produce a consolidated form of the edict, the *Edictum Perpetuum*, removing any scope for radical reform in the future.

LEGISLATION

In comparison with the *ius honorarium* and juristic development, legislation was not an important source of Roman private law. There were exceptions, of course. The *lex Aquilia*, for example, considered in Chapter 8, was a major reform of private law, and the foundation of Roman law, the Twelve Tables, was itself a statute.

The Twelve Tables

Tradition has it that the Twelve Tables were one of the concessions given to the plebeians in the Struggle of the Orders, in this case the demand being for the publication of the law. A commission of ten compiled a statement of the law on ten bronze tablets in 451 BC, a delegation having been sent to study the laws of Greek cities. This perhaps means the Greek cities of southern Italy rather than Greece itself. A further two tablets were added by another commission of ten in 450 BC.

The Twelve Tables were not a law code in the modern sense, being neither comprehensive nor systematic. By no means does the whole law appear, issues of procedure predominating. Subject–matter covered included issues of private, public and religious law. It is unlikely that the Twelve Tables departed much from customary law, despite the story of a delegation to Greek cities. After all, the demand was for the law's publication rather than its reform, and little direct Greek influence can be traced.

The Republican assemblies

In the Republic, formal legislation was the responsibility of the citizen assemblies, the *comitia centuriata*, *comitia tributa* and the *concilium plebis*. The last of these was made up of plebeians, and its legislation, known as *plebiscita*, was initially only binding on them. The assemblies had no legislative initiative. They could only be summoned by the presiding magistrate and vote on proposals put forward by him. Typically, any such proposal would first have been approved by the Senate. The assemblies had, subject to some exceptions, little impact on the development of private law, though they were responsible for some important public law reforms.

In the Empire, consistently with Augustus's reluctance to innovate openly, the assemblies remained in existence and continued to meet when summoned. However, their role was now merely to approve the proposals of the emperor, and by the end of the 1st century AD they had ceased to play an active role.

The Senate

Strictly, the Senate had no legislative power. Its resolutions (*senatusconsulta*) were merely advice to magistrates, with no binding authority of their own, though in practice they were likely to be followed. During the Empire, as the emperor's partners in government, the Senate's resolutions came to be seen as binding, though exactly when this happened is uncertain. Certainly, by the 2nd century AD the process was complete. However, there was no doubt that the emperor was the dominant partner in the relationship, and by the end of the 2nd century there was not even the appearance of initiative left.

The emperor

It was recognised early on that the emperor had the power to legislate. By time of Gaius, it was possible for him to say that there had never been any doubt of this. Thus, the pronouncements (*constitutiones*) of the emperor had binding force. The emperor himself was a magistrate, and so could issue edicts, in his case of universal application. Imperial legislation took various other forms, including *decreta*, judicial decisions in cases heard by the emperor, either at first instance or on appeal, and *rescripta*, written answers to questions or petitions. In practice, these would be written by men who in an earlier age would have been jurists but who were now employed by the State.

THE *CORPUS IURIS CIVILIS*

Time being as it is, the great majority of classical Roman legal works have perished. Almost all of the knowledge we have of classical Roman law comes to us through the *Corpus Iuris Civilis* (Body of Civil Law), the great compilation of Roman law compiled under the instructions of the emperor Justinian in the 6th century. The *Corpus Iuris Civilis* contains four parts, namely the *Institutes*, the *Digest*, the *Codex* and the *Novels*.

The *Codex*

The *Codex*, sometimes Anglicised as "Code", is a collection of prior imperial legislation, compiled in AD 534, and superseding an earlier collection issued in AD 529. The compilation of the *Codex* was assisted by the existence of two unofficial collections from the reign of Diocletian, and an official collection compiled under the instructions of Theodosius II in AD 438.

It should be noted that this is not wholly legislation in the modern sense. As we have seen, the emperor sometimes gave judgments in legal disputes, some emperors being more interested in this than others, and also gave responses to questions and petitions. Because they came from the emperor, such judgments and responses were seen as generally binding, and hence as legislation, and much of the *Codex* is taken up by such matters.

The *Novels*

The *Novels* appear in modern editions of the *Corpus Iuris Civilis* as a collection of subsequent legislation. Such a collection was envisaged, but not actually carried out, by Justinian, and collections appearing in modern editions are derived from unofficial or semi-official collections.

The *Institutes*

Justinian's *Institutes* were an elementary textbook, written by members of the commission that compiled the *Digest*. The book was largely based on the *Institutes* of Gaius, both in terms of content and, especially, structure. Thus, Gaius's Institutional Scheme is adopted with some modifications in Justinian's book. The *Institutes* were issued in AD 533 along with the *Digest*, and were intended as a student's introduction to law, taking up most of the first year of study. The remainder of the student's time, once the basics were mastered, was to be devoted to the study of the *Digest*.

The *Digest*

The major part of the *Corpus Iuris Civilis* is the *Digest*. This is a massive collection of extracts from the writings of classical jurists. The work of compiling the *Digest* was entrusted to a commission headed by Tribonian, one of Justinian's Ministers. In addition to collecting the juristic texts, the commission was instructed to edit them so that they contained nothing obsolete or contradictory. The extent of such alterations to the text, or "interpolations" as they are known, is unclear. At one time it was thought that the *Digest* texts were extensively interpolated, and something of an "interpolation hunt" ensued. A more restrained view is now taken, though interpolations undoubtedly exist.

The work of compiling the *Digest* took 3 years, from AD 530 to AD 533. Justinian tells us that 3,000,000 lines of text were read, and reduced to 150,000 lines. The great majority of the text appearing in the *Digest* was taken from jurists of the years between AD 100 and AD 250.

In contrast with the orderly arrangement of the material in the *Institutes*, there is little in the way of coherent structure in the *Digest*. The *Digest* is arranged into books and titles in the order of the praetor's edict, which evolved haphazardly over time, and so had an essentially arbitrary arrangement of subject-matter.

Within each title, there is a series from extracts from juristic writings, each giving the name of the author and the source text at the beginning. Even these texts are arranged in a way that is apparently arbitrary. The order of the texts was analysed in the 19th century by a German scholar called Bluhme. By noting that texts from the same sources tend to be found in the same order in different titles, Bluhme demonstrated that the work of the commission had been divided between three committees. Each was charged with collecting material from one of three "masses" of texts, named the Sabinian, Edictal and Papinian masses for the first works in each mass. There was also an Appendix mass, perhaps consisting of material that came to light during the process of compilation. The full commission probably only met for a final edit. Without careful editing, this approach will mean that texts dealing with the same issue will often appear far apart within a title, if they happen to be from sources in different masses. In fact, such careful editing was not present, and so the texts appear in a rather haphazard fashion.

Essential Facts

- Much of the development of Roman law came through interpretation by a class of legal experts known as jurists. The jurists wrote extensively on the law, particularly during the "classical" period, ie the late Republic and approximately the first two-and-a-half centuries of the Empire.

- A 2nd-century jurist, Gaius, was responsible for the "Institutional Scheme". This involved dividing the private law into three parts (persons, things and actions), with numerous subclassifications. This approach has been influential into modern law.

- Further development came through the praetor's role in litigation. The praetor would allow new remedies to supplement the civil law. The law created by the praetor was known as the *ius honorarium*.

- Legislation, produced by the citizen assemblies and (during the early Empire) the Senate, was a less important source of law. However, during the Empire, the emperors took an increasingly active role in lawmaking.

- In the 6th century, the emperor Justinian caused a compilation of legal materials, known as the *Corpus Iuris Civilis*, to be made. This comprised the *Institutes* (a student textbook based on a work of the same name by Gaius), the *Digest* (a compilation of juristic writings) and the *Codex* (a collection of imperial pronouncements). Modern editions also include the *Novels*, an unofficial collection of imperial pronouncements dating from after the issue of the *Codex*.

3 THE LAW OF PERSONS

The first part of the tripartite division of private law is the law of persons. As Justinian says, there is "little point in knowing the law if one knows nothing about the persons for whom it exists" (J.1.2.12). Persons, as we shall see, can be classified in various ways, and this affects the way they are treated by the law. The classification of persons depends on their personal status. In modern terms, therefore, the law of persons is the law of personal status, or family law.

STATUS

In Roman law, the status of a Roman citizen was seen as having three elements: *libertas*, or liberty, in that he was not a slave; *civitas*, meaning that he was a Roman citizen; and *familia*, his status as a member of a Roman family. Any of these could change, and this change was called *capitis deminutio*, or status loss.

As there were three elements of status, there were three forms of status loss. Status loss in the first degree (*capitis deminutio maxima*) meant loss of liberty (ie enslavement). This resulted in the loss of citizenship and family membership as well, as a slave could not be a citizen or a member of a Roman family.

Second-degree status loss (*capitis deminutio media*) was loss of *civitas*, which meant loss of *familia* (as one could only be a member of a Roman family if one was a citizen). In this case, though, *libertas* was unaffected, and the person remained free. Status loss of this kind could be imposed as a punishment in various situations.

Third-degree status loss (*capitis deminutio minima*) meant loss of *familia*, but with liberty and citizenship retained. This might happen due to emancipation by the head of the family, the *paterfamilias*. As we shall see, the legal structure of the Roman family was dominated by the *paterfamilias*, to a greater extent even than in other ancient legal systems. The authority of the *paterfamilias* over one of his descendants could be ended by a formal procedure called emancipation. This made the emancipated person legally independent, but at the cost of membership of the family, and consequent loss of succession rights. Emancipation could therefore be used as a punishment for a child, although it does not seem that this was normal. Often, an emancipated son would be given capital by the former *paterfamilias* to set him up in life and to compensate him for the loss of succession rights.

Of the three elements of status, the second, citizenship, tends to be seen as a matter of public law rather than private law. It will therefore be passed over here.

One omission from this treatment of status that may seem surprising is marriage. The reason for this omission is that, in classical Roman law, marriage was notable for its almost complete lack of legal consequences. Marriage is considered further below.

LIBERTAS

The main classification in the law of persons is that between free persons and slaves.

Slavery

As was normal in ancient societies, the Roman economy was dependent on slave labour. Slaves were property, belonging to their master. In early law, the slave's master had the absolute power of life and death over the slave. Although by the time of Justinian this was reduced to a power of reasonable chastisement, for a slave "reasonable chastisement" could doubtless include fairly severe punishments. The slave could not own property, anything acquired by the slave becoming the property of the master.

A person usually became a slave either by being born to a slave woman or through capture in war. Slaves captured in war, at least in earlier times, would often be educated and skilled, and if the war in which the slave was captured was against another Italian state the slave might have a similar cultural background to his Roman masters. Such slaves would often be given responsible jobs. Many professions nowadays considered to carry high status, such as medicine, were in Rome carried out by slaves. On the other hand, slaves coming from the "barbarian" peoples of the north would not usually be thought suited to anything other than manual labour. Thus, although all slaves had the same legal status, it is impossible to generalise about the nature of slavery in Roman society. The legal position is misleading in the case of educated and skilled slaves. Such a slave would have a higher value, and so would often receive better treatment, and might rise to a high position in the management of the master's affairs. Much commercial activity was carried on by slaves permitted to act more or less independently of their masters, although with their masters' capital.

A valuable slave might be allowed a fund of money or property to treat as his own, called a *peculium* (considered below). At the other end of the scale, agricultural slaves, with no marketable skills, and who were cheap and easily replaced, might be treated very poorly indeed.

The end of slavery

Slavery could be brought to an end. Sometimes a slave would be allowed to buy his freedom with his *peculium* which, although belonging to the master, was functionally treated as belonging to the slave. Slavery ended by manumission, for which there were various methods. It was very common for slaves to be manumitted in their master's will.

Augustus imposed restrictions on manumission. By the *lex Aelia Sentia* of AD 4, the permission of a council to investigate manumissions was necessary where the master was aged less than 20 or where the slave was under 30. Manumission by an insolvent master was also void. By the *lex Fufia Caninia* of 2 BC, the number of slaves that could be freed by will was restricted to a maximum of 100, with the permitted number in a given case depending on the total number owned by the testator. These restrictions were largely abolished by Justinian.

Perhaps surprisingly, a manumitted slave became a Roman citizen. However, freedmen, as such former slaves are called, were subject to certain duties of respect to their former master. Some of these would be legal duties agreed at the time of manumission, but the most important consequences were social ones. This was unlikely to have been found unduly onerous. Roman society was based on this kind of relationship between patron and client, and there was no one in Rome not subject to someone else's patronage, save only the emperor.

FAMILIA

In modern law, a child is subject to parental authority. This authority lasts until a particular age, at which point the child is considered adult and the parental authority ends. Roman law also had a system of parental (or, more specifically, paternal) authority. However, the Roman system differed from most others in being lifelong and in the extent of the powers it gave to the head of the household, known as the *paterfamilias*.

The authority of the *paterfamilias* is known as *patria potestas*, or simply *potestas*. Those who are subject to the *potestas* of a *paterfamilias* are said to be *alieni iuris* (subject to another's right). Those not subject to the *potestas* of a *paterfamilias* are said to be *sui iuris* (of their own right, ie independent).

The authority of the *paterfamilias* extends to all those of legitimate birth descended from him in the male line. Such a relationship is called an "agnatic" relationship.

Consider the family tree in Figure 1, headed by a *paterfamilias* with two children and two grandchildren:

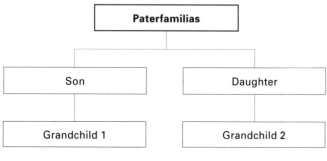

Figure 1

Assuming that the son is married, he, his sister and his own child will all be in the *potestas* of the *paterfamilias*. The daughter is in her father's *potestas* even if she is married, as long as her marriage is the more common marriage *sine manu* (see below). Grandchild 2, on the other hand, will be in the *potestas* of its father or the father's *paterfamilias*. If any of the children are born of unmarried parents, they will be in no one's *potestas*, for *potestas* arises only in the case of offspring of valid civil law marriages.

When the *paterfamilias* in the diagram dies, the son and the daughter will become *sui iuris*. Only a direct ascendant can be a person's *paterfamilias*. Thus, for instance, on the death of the *paterfamilias* in this example, the son does not become his sister's *paterfamilias*. Grandchild 1 will fall into the *potestas* of its father. Grandchild 2 will be unaffected.

Adoption

The rules on *potestas* apply equally to adopted children as to natural children. Equally, adopted children had the same rights of succession to the estate of the *paterfamilias* as did natural children. However, this was changed by Justinian so that, where a child was adopted by someone other than a natural ascendant (whether in the male or female line), there was no change of *potestas*, though rights of succession were acquired in the adoptive family.

There were two forms of adoption: *adoptio* and *adrogatio*. *Adoptio* was the adoption of a person *alieni iuris*, and would involve a formal transfer of *potestas* from the original *paterfamilias* to the adopter. Greater formality was required in the case of *adrogatio*, which was the adoption of a *sui iuris* person. The reason for this is that a *sui iuris* male was a *paterfamilias*, and so his adoption meant the extinction of a Roman family. Accordingly, the adoption would be preceded by an investigation by the *pontifex maximus* (chief priest), and would require to be ratified by the *comitia curiata*.

The powers of the *paterfamilias*

Gaius and Justinian both noted that the powers of the Roman *paterfamilias* were more extensive than those given to fathers elsewhere, both in the extent of the powers of the *paterfamilias* and in their being lifelong. Originally a *paterfamilias* had absolute power of life and death over those in his *potestas*, though this power was gradually restricted. As with slaves, those in *potestas* had no power to own property or to enter into valid contracts. Again as with slaves, though, a child in power could have a *peculium* containing money or property which was treated as belonging to the child, although in fact belonging to the *paterfamilias*.

Leaving aside for now the question of *peculium*, the position of children in *potestas* in respect of property ownership was improved in the Empire. Augustus introduced the *peculium castrense*, allowing sons ownership of any property acquired on military service. The *peculium quasi castrense* of Constantine extended this to all earnings in public service. During the Empire, children also gained the right on their father's death to anything received from the mother or her family, though the property would of course belong to the *paterfamilias* until his death. This property was known as *bona adventicia*, and was eventually extended to include anything received from anyone other than the *paterfamilias*.

The powers of the *paterfamilias* were, moreover, restricted to private law matters. A magistrate could be *alieni iuris*, but had no duty to obey his *paterfamilias* in respect of his public functions.

PECULIUM

The restrictions on ownership of property by persons *alieni iuris* led to practical problems. A person might be of middle years, and might hold high public office, but still be subject to the *potestas* of another. Similarly, a skilled slave might have acquired property, either from the master or through his own efforts. The response to this problem was the recognition of a fund known as the *peculium*. This *peculium* was money or property that the slave or the child in power was allowed to use and dispose of as his own. The *peculium* could be extensive and, for example, a slave's *peculium* might include other slaves with their own *peculia*.

In origin the *peculium* would simply have been a matter of social practice. In law, all property acquired by a child in power or by a slave belonged in law to the *paterfamilias* or master respectively, subject to the exceptions discussed above for children in power. Actions in respect of *peculium* had to be brought by or against the *paterfamilias* or master. It might have been satisfactory in the small agrarian community that was early Rome for the *paterfamilias* to have absolute control of the household's property, particularly given that comparatively short life expectancy would mean that one would usually be released from *potestas* at a fairly young age. This was hardly practical, however, in a major commercial city. And there would always have been long-lived individuals keeping their children in *potestas* into middle age. Some legal recognition for the institution of *peculium* came through praetorian intervention. The praetor introduced actions making it possible to sue the master or *paterfamilias* for the acts of the slave or child in power, though this was restricted to the value of the *peculium* unless the master or *paterfamilias* had authorised the acts in question.

MARRIAGE

Forms of marriage

Two forms of marriage were recognised in Roman law. The older form was marriage *cum manu*, or unfree marriage. In this form of marriage, the wife entered the *potestas* of her husband (or of his *paterfamilias* if her husband was not *sui iuris*). The wife in a marriage *cum manu* was therefore in the position of her husband's daughter, with all that implies for her property. This form of marriage was uncommon by the late Republic.

The more common form of marriage was the free marriage, or marriage *sine manu*. This form of marriage was notable for its comparative lack of legal consequences. Free marriage shared with unfree marriage the consequence that children of the marriage were legitimate. In a free marriage, however, the wife's own status was unaffected. She did not pass into the *potestas* of her husband, and any property she might own did not pass to him. If she was subject to the authority of a *paterfamilias* before the marriage, that remained the case following it.

Comparatively speaking, then, the Roman free marriage had very few consequences. There was no change of *potestas*, there were no consequences for the wife's property or her capacity to contract, and marriage gave the husband no rights over his wife's person. The two most important consequences of marriage were that, other than dowry (considered below), gifts between the spouses were invalid, and that only children of a valid civil law marriage were subject to *patria potestas*.

Formation of marriage

A marriage *cum manu* could be constituted in three ways. The first was *coemptio*, which was in form a bride purchase. This involved a formal conveyance of the bride to the groom, in a manner similar to the method required for transfer of ownership of certain kinds of property (see Chapter 5). The second was *confarreatio*, a religious form of marriage conducted by the *pontifex maximus* and involving the eating of special bread by the parties. The significance of this form was that only children of such marriages were eligible for the higher ranks of the priesthood. By the third form, *usus*, a *manus* marriage was formed by cohabitation for a year with *affectio maritalis*, the consent to be married. To avoid this consequence, it was necessary for the woman to absent herself for three nights in the year.

Marriage *cum manu* was, however, uncommon by the late Republic. By this time, the normal form of marriage was marriage *sine manu*. The constitution of this form of marriage was simple. It required only consent. Neither the customary marriage ceremony nor the cohabitation following it was the determining factor. As the jurist Ulpian says, "it is consent, not sleeping together, which makes a marriage" (D.35.1.15). If either party was *alieni iuris*, the consent of that party's *paterfamilias* would also be required.

In addition to the need for consent, there were various restrictions on the formation of a marriage. The civil law marriage was specific to Roman law, and therefore to Roman citizens. Only Roman citizens (or citizens of communities to which Rome had extended citizenship rights) had the right, called *conubium*, to enter into such a marriage. Marriage was a monogamous union, and so a prior subsisting marriage would be a bar. The parties had to have reached puberty, which was settled as occurring at 14 years of age for boys and 12 for girls. Marriage was also prohibited between close relations, including relationships by adoption or by marriage. From time to time, other restrictions were introduced. For example, under the Twelve Tables, marriages between patricians and plebeians were prohibited, though this ban was soon removed. Soldiers were prohibited from marriage between the reign of Augustus and the repeal of the ban in AD 197 by Septimius Severus. Marriages in contravention of these restrictions were void for all purposes. Thus, for example, a child of an invalid marriage would be illegitimate and would not be subject to *potestas*.

Divorce

There is little evidence of divorce in marriages *cum manu*. It seems to have been rare, and to have involved a formal procedure which would be a variation on the ceremonies for constitution of marriage. By the late Republic, these procedures for divorce appear to have fallen out of use, and the same method was used as for divorce in a marriage *sine manu*.

A marriage *sine manu* was based on the parties' consent, and was ended by the ending of *affectio maritalis*, the consent to be married. This contrasts with medieval and modern law, in which divorce, if allowed at all, is available only on restricted grounds and is an act of the court rather than of the parties. The ending of *affectio maritalis* might be evidenced by the parties ceasing to cohabit, or by the sending of a notice of repudiation by one party to the other. In any case, some objective indication of loss of *affectio maritalis* was necessary. For this reason, a bigamous marriage would not terminate the existing marriage.

By the late Republic, divorce was very common among the upper class, the only part of society for which good evidence is available. Following the adoption of Christianity, attempts to restrict divorce were made, but these were mostly limited to penalising unjust divorces.

Dowry

In Roman marriage, it was normal for a dowry to be given to the groom by or on behalf of the bride, as her contribution to the cost of maintaining the household. The dowry might consist of money or other property, or a combination.

As long as the marriage subsisted, the dowry would be seen as the property of the husband, and therefore his to dispose of as he saw fit. However, as we have seen, divorce was very common. This gave rise to a concern to ensure that the dowry would be returned to the wife if the marriage ended. It became normal, therefore, for the husband to make a binding agreement to restore the dowry on the termination of the marriage. In such a case, the husband was entitled to keep the fruits of the property (ie rents and other profits derived from the property, including natural produce such as crops). The capital, however, would be restored on the termination of the marriage. Alternatively, the husband could agree to return an agreed value for the dowry on termination of the marriage. For cases where no such agreement was made, the praetors introduced an action called the *actio rei uxoriae* (action for the wife's property). This action allowed the wife to sue for return of a fair proportion of the dowry, as determined by the judge.

In the Empire, various reforms were made to the general effect of protecting the wife's position. Augustus prohibited the sale of land forming part of the dowry without the wife's consent, and also the burdening of the land with debts even with the wife's consent. Later, Justinian prohibited sales of such land even with the wife's consent. Augustus did allow, though, the husband to make deductions for necessary expenses, and also made provision for deductions where the wife was guilty or misconduct or had caused the breakdown of the marriage.

GUARDIANSHIP

Potestas was not the only restriction to which a free person might be subject. In addition to *potestas*, certain categories of person were also subject to a guardian (*tutor*) or supervisor (*curator*).

Persons subject to guardianship (*tutela*)

Various categories of person were considered to be in need of protection, although the original purpose of guardianship was to protect those rights of those standing to inherit from the ward. Thus, a person who was insane or a spendthrift might have a guardian appointed. The most important cases were guardianship of *sui iuris* children under puberty and guardianship of women. Plainly, a child under puberty cannot be expected to manage his own affairs, even though he may be *sui iuris*. The special rules for the other important form of guardianship, the guardianship of women, are considered below.

The choice of guardian

In the case of guardianship of children, a guardian could be appointed their father's will. Failing this, there would be appointed a statutory guardian, who was the nearest agnate or (in the case of a manumitted slave or emancipated child) the former master or *paterfamilias*. The reason for this is that, on intestacy, it was the nearest agnate who was entitled to be heir. In the case of an emancipated son, the guardians were the other children of *paterfamilias* who were still in *potestas*, this arising on the death of the *paterfamilias*. Failing these rules, a guardian could also be appointed by the praetor.

The guardian's functions

In the case of a child under puberty, the guardian was responsible for the administration of the child's estate and the authorisation of transactions entered into by the child. Consistent with the origin of guardianship as an institution to protect the interests of the heirs of the child, the guardian was not responsible for the care of the child's person. He was, though, obliged to ensure that the supported and educated in a manner appropriate to his station in life.

Guardianship of women

It has been noted that special rules applied in the case of females. A woman was subject to lifelong guardianship. Attempts were made by the jurists to justify this on the basis of women's weakness of mind. Gaius, however, points out that this is not convincing. In fact, the reason that women's guardianship was lifelong was the same as the reason why guardianship arose in the first place – it is to protect the succession rights of the agnates. A boy's guardianship ends with puberty, because he can then marry and produce children to be his heirs. At that point those who would previously have been his heirs have no further interest in the matter. A woman's children, however, are not her heirs according to the general law of succession. The reason for this is that they have no agnatic relationship to her. Thus, the interest of her agnates in her estate is lifelong. For this reason, a woman's husband would not be her guardian, and a guardian could be appointed even for a married woman.

Guardianship of women was also special in having a restricted purpose. Where the guardian of a child was also responsible for the administration of his property, the guardian of a woman was restricted to giving consent to her transactions. This consent could often be compelled, and during the Empire women's guardianship became almost devoid of content. Indeed, by a reform of Augustus, a woman who had had at least three children (four if a freedwoman) was released from guardianship.

Liability of a guardian

A guardian was liable for fraud or negligence in the conduct of his duties. Except in cases of appointment by will or by the praetor, where it would be assumed that consideration had been given to the guardian's suitability, the guardian would normally need to provide security for such liability. An action could be brought for removal of an untrustworthy guardian, although this remedy was not available to the ward himself. The ward himself had to wait until the end of the guardianship to sue. The praetor could also intervene in the guardianship to give directions to the guardian, if asked.

Supervision of minors (*cura minorum*)

While guardianship of a boy ended at puberty, such a child was still not fully capable of managing his own affairs. Accordingly, the *lex Plaetoria*, introduced around 200 BC, penalised fraud against those past puberty, up to an age at which they could be seen as capable of managing their own affairs, which was taken to be 25. The praetors extended this protection by providing a defence to the enforcement of a contract disadvantageous to the minor, even in the absence of fraud. For this reason, the practice developed of requiring the appointment of a supervisor for such transactions, the purpose of the supervisor being to supply consent to transactions entered into by the ward. This had the effect of protecting third parties contracting with minors, and a supervisor could be appointed on an *ad hoc* or continuing basis.

Essential Facts

- The main element of a person's legal status was the division between free persons and slaves. Slaves were the property of their masters, and could not themselves own any property. They might, however, be allowed a *peculium*, ie a fund of property they were allowed to treat as their own.

- The most distinctive feature of the Roman family was the authority over his descendants of the *paterfamilias*, ie the oldest male ascendant in the male line. Subject to a few exceptions, no one subject to this authority was able to own any property. Such a person might, however, be allowed a *peculium* in much the same way as a slave.

- The common form of marriage from the late Republic onwards was the free marriage, or marriage *sine manu*. In this form of marriage, the wife's property rights were not affected and she remained subject to the authority of her *paterfamilias* if she had one. She did not become subject to the legal authority of her husband. The older unfree marriage, or marriage *sine manu*, by contrast broke the wife's legal ties with her family, and put her under her husband's authority.

- Those not subject to the authority of a *paterfamilias* were subject to the supervision of a guardian (*tutor*) up to the age of puberty (for males) or for life (for females). Males up to the age of 25, however, could have a *curator* appointed to supervise them in entering into legal transactions.

Essential Cases

Mackenzie v Mackenzie's Trs (1916): this case concerns one of the irregular forms of marriage recognised in Scots common law – the marriage by words of present consent. The irregular forms of marriage were ultimately derived, through canon law (see Chapter 11), from the Roman idea of marriage by consent. In this case, the court held that there was a valid marriage where a man had given a written acknowledgement of marriage to his servant. This was the case even though she continued to act as a servant, for the sake of public appearances. This form of marriage was abolished by the Marriage (Scotland) Act 1939.

X v Y (1921): this case concerned another of the common-law irregular marriages – the marriage by future consent followed by intercourse. In this case, a man and woman were engaged and, during the engagement, had sexual intercourse. The court said that "where a girl hitherto pure and innocent has intercourse with a man to whom she is engaged to be married, the presumption is that the engagement to marry was relied upon in consenting to the intercourse. The law presumes that in such circumstances consent to intercourse is consent to immediate marriage". This form of marriage was abolished by the Marriage (Scotland) Act 1939.

Gow v Lord Advocate (1993): this case concerned the irregular form of marriage known as marriage by cohabitation with habit and repute. The idea behind this form of marriage was that the parties impliedly consented by holding themselves out as married. In this case, the action failed because there was insufficient repute of marriage. This form of marriage was abolished by the Family Law (Scotland) Act 2006.

4 THE LAW OF THINGS: RIGHTS IN PROPERTY

Property law is part of the law of things, the second part of Gaius' Institutional Scheme (see Chapter 2). The law of things, it will be remembered, includes property law, the law of obligations and the law of succession. In the Institutional Scheme, property law is divided into corporeal things (*res corporales*) and incorporeal things (*res incorporales*). The category of corporeal property covers things with a physical existence, and incorporeal property things with no physical existence (in other words, rights – such as a right to payment of a debt or a right to occupy land under a usufruct). What all these have in common is that they are all assets, all items of property. Thus, property law in its broadest sense includes the law of obligations. However, although the right created for example by a contract is an item of (incorporeal) property, it is customary to treat the rules for the creation of rights arising from the law of obligations and the law of succession separately from the consideration of real rights.

CLASSIFICATION OF PROPERTY

There are various ways in which Roman law classified property. We have seen that, in the first place, Roman law distinguished between corporeal and incorporeal property.

Property was also classified in other ways. As in modern law, a distinction was made between moveable and immoveable property (*res mobiles* and *res immobiles*), immoveable property meaning land and things attached to land, such as buildings. This distinction was much less important than it is in modern law.

In classical Roman law, a distinction was also made between *res mancipi* and *res nec mancipi*, the former being property requiring particular formal methods of transfer (see Chapter 5) until the distinction was abolished by Justinian. Property falling into the category of *res nec mancipi* could be transferred or (in the case of incorporeal property) created informally. The category of *res mancipi* was made up of slaves, certain beasts of burden (oxen, horses, asses and mules), Italic land and rustic praedial servitudes (see below) over such land. The origin of the distinction is unclear, but it has been suggested that these types of property were marked out in the early period as important in agriculture. By the late Republic, in any case, the list became fixed, and beasts of burden (such as camels) which became known to the Romans later did not enter the list of *res mancipi*.

REAL RIGHTS AND PERSONAL RIGHTS

One of the things that are most characteristic of a legal system based on Roman law is the distinction between real rights (including ownership) and personal rights. In short, the distinction is this: a personal right is enforceable only against a particular person or particular persons; a real right is enforceable against anyone. Thus, if I own a horse which is then stolen (ownership being a real right), I will be able to recover the horse from anyone into whose hands it comes. This is the case even if that person has no knowledge of the theft. On the other hand, if I have merely agreed to buy the horse from you, as we shall see in Chapter 5, I do not acquire ownership until the property has been conveyed to me. Until that point I have only a personal right, arising from my contract with you. On the basis of that personal right, I can compel you to deliver the horse to me. However, if you sell to a third party, I will not be able to compel that third party to deliver the property to me. The reason for this is that my right, being a personal right only, is enforceable only against the other party to the obligation (ie you).

The distinction between real and personal rights arises from a distinction made in the law of actions between real actions (*actiones in rem*) and personal actions (*actiones in personam*). In a real action, the party bringing the action (the *actor*, or "pursuer" in modern Scots terminology) is asserting a relationship with the property that is the subject-matter of the litigation, namely that he owns it. In a personal action, the *actor* is asserting a relationship with another party, namely the other party to the action. Of this type is the *condictio*, the basic personal action. In the *condictio*, the *actor* claimed that he was owed a specific debt or item of property by the other party. From this distinction arises the idea that a personal action can be brought only against the other party to the obligation concerned, whereas a real action could be brought against any person acting in such a way as to deny the *actor*'s title to the property.

Only a limited number of real rights were recognised by the law. The remainder of this chapter considers the most important of these.

OWNERSHIP

The nature of ownership

In Roman law and those systems based on it, ownership is recognised as absolute: a "distinct paramount right" (E Metzger (ed), *A Companion to Justinian's Institutes*, p 45), rather than being a relative concept. In relation to an item of property, there will be an identifiable right of ownership.

With the exception of possession (for possession is not dependent on having any entitlement to possess), all other real rights are derived from the owner. Ownership is the right one has in one's own property. The other real rights are rights in someone else's property (*iura in re aliena*). Ownership is thus qualitatively different from the other real rights, being the residual real right that remains when all other rights in the property fall.

The rights of the owner

This is not to say that the rights of an owner are unrestricted. My right to use my property is restricted by my neighbour's right to undisturbed enjoyment of his property. There may be rights affecting the property, possibly to the extent that I have no right to present enjoyment of the property. A lease or a usufruct, for example, will leave me with no present right to occupy the property. However, if and when those rights expire, I will be able to resume occupation.

Ownership has been defined as the *ius utendi, fruendi, abutendi* – the right of use, enjoyment and abuse. Usually, no one will have the right to use, enjoy or damage the property without deriving their right to do so from the owner.

Bonitary ownership

To the principle that ownership is absolute, there is one exception. As noted above, ownership of certain kinds of property (called *res mancipi*) could be transferred only by particular formal modes of conveyance. Any attempt to transfer ownership of *res mancipi* using another method would be unsuccessful, leaving the transferor as owner. However, such informal transfers were common, leading to the praetor giving protection to the transferee in such cases. These praetorian reforms left the transferor as owner according to the civil law, but gave remedies to the transferee equivalent to those of an owner. The view was eventually taken that the right of the transferee in such a case was a form of ownership. This right was called "bonitary ownership" because, although not owner according to the civil law, the possessor had the property *in bonis* (among his goods). Only Gaius appears to have recognised this as a form of ownership, however.

The concept of bonitary ownership became redundant on Justinian's abolition of the category of *res mancipi*, such property then being capable of transfer by the ordinary methods.

POSSESSION

The nature of possession

Possession is a distinct real right, with, as the jurist Ulpian says, "nothing in common with possession" (D.41.2.12). As Nicholas says:

> "There is an obvious distinction in ordinary language between having a thing and being entitled to it. The thief is not entitled to what he has stolen but he nevertheless has it, and conversely the man who has pawned his ring is still entitled to it but the pawnbroker actually has it." (*An Introduction to Roman Law*, p 107)

This distinction, between ownership and possession, is fundamental to understanding Roman property law. However, it is not always easy to understand whether a person is in possession of property.

Acquisition and loss of possession

There are two elements in possession: the physical (*corpus*) and the mental (*animus*), and possession is acquired when the two coincide:

> "Now we take possession physically and mentally, not mentally alone or physically alone." (Paul, D.41.2.3.1)

The physical element of possession requires some degree of physical control over the property. This control need not, however, be absolute. Thus, in the case of land, possession of a part will be equivalent to possession of the whole.

Mere physical holding, however, will not give possession in itself. One must also hold the property with the necessary state of mind. One must usually have the intention to hold the property as owner – one must have *animus domini*. However, some other holders, such as creditors holding debtors' property on pledge, were also classed as possessors. On the other hand, a usufructuary did not have possession. The rationale for this is not entirely clear.

The juristic writings in the *Digest*, likewise, do not give a clear rule on how possession is lost. Characteristically, the jurists consider the matter on a case-by-case basis. There was a rule that there could not be more than one right of possession of the same property at the same time. If you take possession of my land, I lose possession, although the view appears to have been taken that I do not lose possession in this case until I find out and fail to eject you. Otherwise, the jurist Paul says:

"Just as no possession can be acquired except physically and with intent, so none is lost unless both elements are departed from." (Paul, D.41.2.8)

However, there are texts contradicting this. For example, it is stated elsewhere that one can lose possession of a thing by losing the intention to possess even though physical control is retained. An example of this might be if I sell my land to you but we agree that I will remain as a tenant. As a tenant does not have possession in Roman law, I would lose possession in this case.

The rights of the possessor

Possession is significant because it has consequences in the law, most notably in being protected. As with the distinction between real and personal rights, this again arises from the rules of procedure. If there is a dispute over who is entitled to a particular piece of property, it will be necessary to decide who is to retain the property pending resolution of the dispute. Usually, the party with possession would be left in possession until the dispute was resolved. However, it is possible that the other party would try to pre-empt the legal process by seizing possession. In order to avoid such action, the law introduced various remedies to protect the possessor. The general effect of these was that, as long as the possessor had not acquired possession *vi, clam aut precario* (by force, stealth or licence) from the other party, he was entitled to retain possession until a better right to the property could be shown. If he was dispossessed, he was entitled to be restored to possession pending legal proceedings.

However, this remedy was available only against the dispossessor: as we have seen, by the act of dispossession possession is lost, and with it the possessory remedies. Thus, if the dispossessor sold the property to a third party, the original party dispossessed would have no remedy against that third party, on the basis of his possession.

If in good faith, the possessor was also entitled to retain any fruits of the property as long as good faith lasted. By "fruits" is meant both natural fruits (*fructus naturales*), such as things growing on land and the young of animals, and civil fruits (*fructus civiles*), meaning rents and other profits derived from the property. If he made any improvements to the property, the good-faith possessor was entitled to retain the property until he was compensated for his expenses. If the property was damaged through some person's fault, the good-faith possessor was entitled to an action under the *lex Aquilia* (see Chapter 8) for the loss of the value of these rights.

PRAEDIAL SERVITUDES

Nature of praedial servitudes

It will often be the case that it is desirable for neighbours to agree that one can make some use of the other's land, or that one will not use his land in a particular way. One way of achieving this is the creation of a praedial servitude. A praedial servitude is a right against the owner of one area of land, the servient property, held by the owner of neighbouring land, the dominant property, restricting in some way the servient owner's enjoyment of his property. Of course, one could achieve this effect by contract. A contract, though, gives only a personal right. Thus, if the servient owner sold his land, the new owner would not be bound by the contract. A servitude, on the other hand, is a real right, and will bind successors of the servient owner.

A praedial servitude is more than this, though. In addition to binding successors of the servient owner, the benefit of the servitude passes with ownership of the dominant land. Thus, if I have a servitude right of way over your land, and I sell my land, the new owner will acquire the right of way along with ownership of the land. This is the reason these rights are called "praedial" servitudes (from the Latin *praedium*, meaning an estate of land): because they can be held only by someone who owns land.

A praedial servitude exists for the benefit of the dominant owner. However, the dominant owner is restricted in the benefit he can take. The benefit taken must relate to the dominant property in some way. Thus, for example, a right to fish on your land would not benefit me in my capacity as owner of neighbouring land: a non-owner would benefit just as much. Accordingly, this would not be a valid servitude. Equally, if I had a servitude right to take building materials from your land, I could use those materials only on the dominant land. I could not sell them to others, for example, because then I would be taking a benefit that did not relate to the dominant land.

An important restriction as to the content of a praedial servitude was that it could not require any action on the part of the servient owner. This restricted praedial servitudes to two options: either allowing the dominant owner to make some use of the servient property (as with a right of access); or prohibiting some action by the servient owner (as where the servient owner is prohibited from building).

Classification and types of praedial servitude

Various types of praedial servitude were recognised. A distinction was made between urban and rustic praedial servitudes. This distinction did not relate to the location of the land, but to the type of land affected by the servitude. If the servient property was a building, the servitude would be urban; otherwise, it would be rustic. Thus, a servitude burdening a farmhouse would be an urban servitude.

Among the most common types of rustic praedial servitude was the right of access. This gives the dominant owner the right to take access over the servient property to get to his own property. This servitude came in three forms: *iter*, which was for pedestrian access only; *actus*, which also extended to livestock; and *via*, which included vehicular access. A rustic servitude could also be created giving the right to lead water over the servient land (the servitude of *aquaeductus*) or to draw water from the servient land. Other rustic servitudes included rights to water or pasture livestock, to dig sand or to burn lime.

One of the more common types of urban servitude was the right of support. This could take the form either of requiring a building on the servient land to bear the weight of a building on the dominant land (the servitude *oneris ferendi*) or of allowing the dominant owner to put out a supporting beam into the servient building (the servitude *tigni immittendi*). Other types included rights of drainage and rights to light, prohibiting the servient owner building above a certain level.

PERSONAL SERVITUDES

In addition to the praedial servitudes, there was also a category of personal servitudes. In this case, the benefit of the servitude was held by an individual personally, rather than in his capacity as owner of land.

Nature of usufruct

A usufruct is the right to the use and fruits of corporeal property, whether land or moveables. It is most commonly created as a legacy and lasts for the lifetime of the usufructuary (the holder of the usufruct). As the property is to be restored intact to the owner at the termination of the usufruct, a usufruct cannot be created over perishable property or property that is consumed by use (such as food or drink). An exception is made, however, in the case of money, as long as the usufructuary gives security for the return to the owner of the same amount of money.

Rights and obligations of the parties

As noted, the owner of the property is entitled to have the property restored to him at the end of the usufruct. Accordingly, the usufructuary is bound to maintain the property and is not permitted to encroach on the substance of the property, for example by cutting down trees or demolishing buildings. The usufructuary is, however, entitled to take the fruits of the property.

Related rights

Three other personal servitudes were recognised. *Usus* was like usufruct, but without the right to the fruits of the property. *Habitatio* and *operae servorum* were similar to *usus*, but related to houses and the services of slaves respectively.

RIGHTS IN SECURITY

Suppose that a debtor owes money to a creditor. The creditor has a personal right against the debtor, which he can use to recover the debt through legal proceedings. However, this may not be enough to ensure recovery of the debt. The debtor may be insolvent, and so have insufficient assets to pay off all of his debtors. To allow a creditor to improve his chances of payment, the law allows the creation of rights in security.

A real right in security is a right in an item of the debtor's property given to the creditor to secure payment of the debt. It may give the creditor the right to sell the property in order to pay off the debt. As Justinian observes (J.3.14.4), a right in security "benefits both parties, the debtor because it helps him get credit, and the creditor because it helps him give credit safely". Justinian is speaking here specifically about the right in security called pledge, but the same is true for any security right.

A right is security is a right accessory to the debt. What this means is that the security right is dependent for its existence on the existence of the debt, but the debt is not dependent for its existence on the right in security. Thus, if the debt is paid off, the right in security is also extinguished. On the other hand, if the right in security is lost for some reason, that does not affect the debtor's obligation to pay the debt.

Pledge (*pignus*)

Pledge was a right in security over corporeal property, constituted by delivery of the property by the pledgor (debtor) to the pledgee (creditor). For the requirements of delivery, see Chapter 5. The right of pledge was dependent on continued possession by the creditor. Accordingly, if possession was lost for any reason, the creditor's real right would be lost, although, as mentioned, the debt would continue to be payable.

Rights and obligations of the pledgee

The creditor, having possession of the debtor's property, was under an obligation to take care of the property, as Justinian says, to "the highest standard of care" (J.3.14.4). He would therefore be liable to the debtor for any damage caused to the property because of failure to meet this standard of care. The creditor would not, however, be liable for any damage occurring without fault on his part.

Originally, pledge gave the creditor no right to sell the property, only the right to retain it. However, it became common practice to contract for an express power of sale, to the extent that in the classical period a power of sale was taken to be implied unless expressly contracted out of.

Other rights in security

Various other forms of security were recognised. Not all of these are real rights in security in the strict sense described above, in that not all gave the creditor a *ius in re aliena*.

Fiducia

This was the original form of security. It involved a formal conveyance of the property to the creditor subject to an obligation to reconvey on repayment. *Fiducia* therefore gave the creditor ownership rather than a *ius in re aliena*. This made the debtor vulnerable to the creditor transferring the property to a third party.

Hypotheca

This evolved from pledge, and was a right in security which allowed the debtor to retain possession. It therefore gave the advantage to the debtor that he was not deprived of the use of the property. However, in the absence of a system of public registration of security rights (as is found in most modern systems), the creditor was subject to the disadvantage that he could not be sure whether a previous *hypotheca* had been created over the property. This might have the effect of making the security worthless, because those creditors with securities created earlier would be paid first. If the value of the property was insufficient to pay off all secured creditors, those with securities created later might recover little or nothing.

Personal security

It was also possible for the creditor to secure his position, not by acquiring a real right in something belonging to the debtor, but by a third party guaranteeing payment of the debt. This was done by means of a form of *stipulatio* (see Chapter 7) known as *adpromissio*. The third party would undertake to pay off the debt if the debtor failed to pay. In other words, the third party acts as a guarantor of the debt or, in modern Scots terminology, a cautioner.

Essential Facts

- Property law is part of the second division in the Institutional Scheme. Property rights can be divided into real rights and personal rights. A real right is a right in an item of property, and can be enforced against anyone interfering with that property. A personal right is enforceable only against a particular person or persons. Real rights are part of the law of property in the narrower sense, whereas personal rights are the province of the law of obligations. Only a limited number of real rights were recognised.

- The main real right was ownership, which was the ultimate power of using and disposing of a thing. In principle, there could be only one right of ownership in an item of property. However, a person who had taken by an inappropriate method of conveyance property falling into the category known as *res mancipi* was given some of the rights of an owner, and was known as "bonitary owner".

- A person in possession of property, even without a right to possess, was entitled to remain in possession until the question of right was resolved. The real right of possession was lost if the possessor was dispossessed but if this happened the dispossessed party had a personal right against the dispossessor for the property's return. If in good faith (ie if he believed he had a right to the property), the possessor had also several other rights, particularly the right to retain the fruits of the property as long as good faith lasted.

- Praedial servitudes were rights held by the owner of one area of land (the dominant land) to make some specified use of a neighbour's land (the servient land) or to restrict in some way the neighbour's use of his land. Because the servitude was a real right, it bound any subsequent owner of the servient land. The benefit of the servitude also passed to any subsequent owner of the dominant land.

- Usufruct was the most important of the class of real rights known as personal servitudes. This entitled the holder to the use and enjoyment of property usually for life. The usufructuary was entitled to the fruits of the property but could not diminish its substance, for example by demolishing buildings.

- A right in security was a right subsidiary to an obligation, with the purpose of securing payment of the obligation. The main real rights in security were pledge, which involved the creditor having possession of an item of the debtor's property, and hypothec, which did not.

Essential Cases

Burnett's Tr v Grainger (2004): Mrs Burnett entered into a contract to sell a house to the Graingers, who paid the purchase price. However, before the real right of ownership could be transferred to the Graingers, Mrs Burnett's estate was sequestrated (ie she was declared bankrupt). Her property was transferred to a trustee, who took title to the house. The court held that, as the Graingers had only a personal right at this time, they could not enforce this right against the trustee. The trustee was accordingly entitled to the house.

Stronach's Exrs v Robertson (2002): Mr Robertson held a liferent (the Scots equivalent of a usufruct) over a house, which it was alleged he had allowed to fall into disrepair. The owners sought to compel him to make repairs. With reference to Roman authority, Mr Robertson successfully argued that he could not be compelled to make repairs, but only to provide security for the damage.

Moncrieff v Jamieson (2008): this case discussed the question whether it was possible to have a servitude right allowing the parking of a car on the servient land. It was accepted that this was competent. Roman authority was discussed in the House of Lords in support of this proposition.

5 THE LAW OF THINGS: ACQUISITION OF OWNERSHIP

The last chapter looked at the real rights in property that were recognised in Roman law. We turn now to how the real right of ownership is acquired.

CLASSIFICATION OF MODES OF ACQUISITION

Modes of acquisition can be classified in various ways. For example, Roman law classified modes of acquisition according to whether they arose from the *ius gentium* (the law of peoples or nations) or the *ius civile* (civil law, ie Roman law). The point of this distinction is that the *ius civile* methods of acquisition were open only to Roman citizens. Another distinction is between original acquisition and derivative acquisition. Derivative acquisition occurs when ownership is acquired from a previous owner. Original acquisition occurs when property is acquired otherwise than from a previous owner, as, for example, with the acquisition of ownerless property. In original acquisition, the acquirer takes ownership unaffected by any defect in the right of any previous owner. In derivative acquisition, on the other hand, the acquirer's right is subject to any such defect. Thus, for example, a buyer of stolen property (who would acquire by derivative acquisition) gains no right to the property, as the seller had no such right.

DERIVATIVE ACQUISITION

Mancipatio

Mancipatio was a formal method of transfer used for property falling into the category of *res mancipi* (see Chapter 4). It required the presence of five witnesses, plus a sixth person called a *libripens* who held a set of bronze scales. The transferee held the property to be transferred in one hand and a piece of bronze in the other. He then made a formal declaration of ownership and struck the scales with the bronze, which was then handed to the transferor to represent the price. Despite this symbolical payment in bronze, the transfer need not be a sale.

We saw in Chapter 4 that the praetor developed protections for a person who had taken *res mancipi* without a formal transfer. For this reason, *mancipatio* as a form of transfer was obsolete even before the distinction between *res mancipi* and *res nec mancipi* was abolished by Justinian.

In iure cessio

As an alternative to *mancipatio*, transfer could be effected by a process known as *in iure cessio*. This involved the parties going before the praetor. The transferee would make a formal claim to the property to be transferred, which the transferor would decline to oppose. The praetor would then adjudge the property to be the transferee's. Compared with *mancipatio*, this had the disadvantage of having to go before the praetor. For this reason, *in iure cessio* was typically used only for incorporeal property.

Traditio

The usual method of transfer of property was *traditio*, which is generally translated by the term "delivery". This involved the transfer of possession from the transferor to the transferee, and was used both for moveable property and for land. This mode of transfer was received into Scots law for the transfer of moveable property, although its scope is now limited by the Sale of Goods Act 1979 to transfers other than those resulting from a sale (ie gifts and exchanges).

The simplest form of delivery was an actual delivery into the transferee's personal custody. The requirement was a transfer of possession. We saw in Chapter 4 that possession meant physical control of the property accompanied by an intention to possess. As possession could be held through another, such as a slave, it was sufficient that delivery was made to someone acting on the transferee's behalf.

Several other forms of delivery were recognised. It was enough to deliver the keys of the repository in which the property was kept, this being sufficient to give the transferee control and therefore possession of the goods. This method was known as *traditio clavium* (delivery of keys).

Valid delivery could be made where the transferor intended the property to belong to the first person who picked it up, this being called *traditio incertae personae* (delivery to an uncertain person). An example of this would be a politician seeking election throwing coins to a crowd. Whichever member of the crowd picked up a coin would become its owner.

Traditio longa manu was a valid form of delivery, which took place where property difficult or impossible to move was being transferred. It involved the transferor pointing out the property to the transferee and permitting the latter to take possession. Thus, the jurists tell us that, where the boundaries of land to be transferred were pointed out to the transferee from a tower on neighbouring land, that was valid delivery even without the transferee actually entering into physical possession.

Because the point of *traditio* was a transfer of possession, there was no need for a physical transfer where the transferee already had physical custody of the property. Thus, for example, where land was sold to a sitting tenant, the tenant became owner as soon as (with the transferor's consent) he had the intention to possess the land as owner. This form of delivery was called *traditio brevi manu*. There was no need in such a case for the tenant or other holder to hand the property back to the owner in order for it to be redelivered.

It has been noted that possession could be held through another. Suppose that there is an agreement that the transferee will become owner, but the transferor will continue to have custody of the property. The transferee is to possess through the transferor. Would this be a valid delivery? The following text of the jurist Celsus suggests that this was possible:

> "What I possess in my own name I can possess in that of another ... I cease to possess and make the other person possessor through my agency. For it is one thing to possess and another to possess on someone else's behalf; he is the possessor in whose name a thing is possessed; the procurator simply provides the agency of another's possession." (D.41.2.18pr)

An example would be where A sold land to B, but remained in occupation as a tenant. The scope of this *constitutum possessorium*, as it is called, is controversial. There is certainly sufficient in the texts to allow its recognition to be inferred, at least in some circumstances, but the name "*constitutum possessorium*" itself is a medieval invention and does not appear anywhere in the Roman sources. The problem with it is that it appears to undermine the requirement for delivery. It would appear that *constitutum possessorium* was accepted as valid only where there was some proper legal ground for the retention of custody by the transferor, such as a lease.

Iusta causa

It was said that delivery was valid only if it had some proper legal basis justifying the transfer of ownership. This was known as a *iusta causa*, or just cause, such as a sale or a gift. The nature of this requirement is not precisely clear, but it appears that its role was merely to provide "evidence of the parties' intention that ownership should pass, [and] did not need to have an objective existence" (E Metzger (ed), *Companion to Justinian's Institutes*, p 53). For this reason, it appears that ownership passed even if the parties were in disagreement as to the *causa* of the transfer:

> "When we indeed agree on the thing delivered but differ over the grounds of delivery, I see no reason why the delivery should not be effective; an example would be that I think myself bound under a will to transfer land to you and you think that it is due under a stipulation. Again, if I give you coined money as a gift and you receive it as a loan, it is settled law that the fact that we disagree on the grounds of delivery and acceptance is no barrier to the transfer of ownership to you." (Julian, D.41.1.36)

In the examples given by Julian, ownership passes because the parties both intend it to pass. In the case where one party believes the money is a loan and the other a gift, both intend ownership to pass. The reason that there is such an intention in the case of a loan of money is that Roman law recognised two distinct types of loan. Where the loan was for consumption, as with money or food, for example, ownership passed and the borrower was bound to return the value. In a loan for use, the same property was to be returned and ownership did not pass to the borrower. This matter is considered further in Chapter 7.

If the parties disagreed on the *causa* of the transfer, it might be that the transfer could be challenged in court. Someone who received money believing it to be a gift where the other believed it to be a loan would be liable to return the money on the ground of unjustified enrichment (see Chapter 9). But until that was done, the transferee remained the owner. Such a transferee could, for example, transfer ownership to a third party. Such a third party, knowing nothing of the previous transaction, would acquire a right to the property that was entirely unchallengeable.

ORIGINAL ACQUISITION

Occupatio

The remaining forms of acquisition to be considered are all forms of original acquisition.

In some cases, it was possible to acquire ownership of property merely by taking possession of it. This was known as *occupatio*. *Occupatio* applied to three categories of property. The first was property that had never been owned, such as pebbles on a beach or a new island rising in the sea.

The second category was property that had once been owned but was no longer owned. This category included abandoned property, and also wild animals that had escaped from their owner. As we shall see, escaped wild animals revert to an ownerless state. The third category was enemy property captured in wartime.

This doctrine applies in modern Scots law, although in restricted form. In modern law, only ownerless wild animals and things that have never been owned are open to acquisition by *occupatio*. Abandoned property and land that has no previous owner are excluded from acquisition by *occupatio* in modern Scots law as belonging to the Crown.

Most practical problems in *occupatio* arise in relation to the ownership of wild animals. There appears to have been a dispute in early law about how ownership of an animal was taken. Suppose that a hunter has wounded an animal, and is pursuing it. Before he catches it, another hunter intercepts the animal and takes it. Which of the two obtains ownership? Some jurists thought that actual physical seizure was necessary, which would mean that the second hunter would acquire ownership. Others, though, thought that one acquired ownership of an animal by pursuing it, which would favour the first hunter. By Justinian's time, however, it was settled that actual capture of the animal was necessary. The animal belonged, therefore, to the first person to lay hands on the animal or in some way to confine it (in a trap or snare, for example). This was the case even where the animal was caught on someone else's land.

To maintain ownership of a wild animal, it was necessary to maintain control. If control was lost, ownership was lost. This might be done by keeping the animal confined. Alternatively, an animal might be kept unconfined if it was tamed or had a habit of returning (such as a homing pigeon). In such a case, ownership was maintained as long as the animal remained tame or retained its habit of returning. Ownership was lost only when the animal reverted to its wild state (unless it was confined) or lost the habit of returning. Where control was maintained only by confinement, and the animal escaped confinement, ownership was maintained as long as the owner was in pursuit with a reasonable prospect of recapture.

It should be noted that these rules applied only to wild species of animal. Tame species were treated in the same way as any other moveable property. Thus, an escaped cat or dog did not become ownerless.

Specificatio

Suppose that a person takes materials belonging to another and makes a new thing from it. This new thing is known as a *nova species*. The classic example is the transformation of grapes into wine. Who owns the wine in this case?

There was a dispute in classical law between the Sabinians and the Proculians over the correct answer to this question. The Sabinians took the view that the new thing belonged to the owner of the materials. The Proculians, on the other hand, would have given ownership to the manufacturer. Justinian resolved the issue by taking a middle course. He made the answer to the question depend on whether the new thing could be restored to its original form. If the thing could be restored to its original form, it remained the property of its original owner. If it could not be restored to its original form, it became the property of the maker, although he might be liable to compensate the owner of the materials. Thus, a gold statue would belong to the owner of the materials (because the gold could be melted down and put back into its original form), but a marble statue would belong to the maker. This is also the position followed in modern Scots law.

This could, of course, be excluded by the parties' agreement. Thus, if a new thing is manufactured by an employee on behalf of his employer, there is no doubt that the new thing belongs to the employer.

Accessio

Where two things are permanently joined together, the lesser (or accessory), object becomes part of the greater (or principal) object. By the principle of *accessio*, the accessory is said to "accede" to the principal. The owner of the principal acquires ownership of the accessory, although in some circumstances he will be bound to compensate the owner of the accessory. This is the modern Scots position, and was also law for the Romans.

There may sometimes be difficulty with accession in determining which item is the principal and which the accessory. In the case of land, however, the matter was simple enough. Where there was union between moveable property and land, the land was the principal. Thus, a building acceded to the land, as did a plant when it took root. In the case of the building, however, the, perhaps surprising, rule appears to have developed that the original owner retained ownership of the materials of which the building was made, though he could not retrieve them unless the building was demolished.

Where there was a union between moveables, there was greater difficulty in determining which was the principal. Unfortunately, no single, clear test appears in the Roman texts. One that was used was relative value of the objects, but that was not conclusive. Thus, even gold lettering accedes to the page it is written on. A particular example that is difficult to account for under any principle was that, where a person painted on another's canvas, the canvas acceded to the painting, even though the painting could not exist without the canvas.

Commixtio and confusio

Commixtio and *confusio* are both concerned with the situation where property belonging to two or more people is mixed together in such a way that the property of one cannot be distinguished from the other. *Commixtio* applies where solids are mixed, as where two herds of sheep are mingled together. *Confusio* applies in the case of liquids or gases, as where two bottles of wine are mixed. In both cases, the effect is co-ownership among those who owned the components of the mix, in proportion to their contribution. The rule is the same in modern Scots law.

Usucapio

How does one prove ownership of the property in one's possession? In practice, of course, it will readily be presumed that the possessor is the owner, but this only takes the matter so far. It does not eliminate the possibility that the property may in fact belong to someone else, who may emerge to claim the property from someone who has bought it in good faith from a non-owner. This is a problem that all legal systems must face. In modern Scots law, the problem is dealt with (for land, at least) by means of positive prescription, now regulated by the Prescription and Limitation (Scotland) Act 1973. The 1973 Act, provided that certain criteria are satisfied, gives ownership to a person who has possessed the land for a specified period of time, currently 10 years. This means that ownership of the land need not be investigated beyond this period. English law achieves much the same effect through the doctrine of adverse possession. This idea also appeared in Roman law under the name of *usucapio*. This is the final form of original acquisition to be considered.

Like *mancipatio* and *in iure cessio*, *usucapio* was a *ius civile* mode of acquisition, and so was open only to Roman citizens. The purpose of *usucapio* was to reduce the possibility of doubts as to ownership by allowing a possessor of property to acquire ownership through the passage of time. In this case, the possessor has property belonging to another person. On the expiry of the relevant period of time for *usucapio*, that person loses ownership and the possessor gains ownership.

One of the most important cases to which *usucapio* was applied in the classical law was the acquisition of *res mancipi*. It will be remembered that this category of property, which included such things as slaves, livestock and land in Italy, required special formal methods of transfer. However, in practice this was often disregarded, no doubt on the basis that it was inconvenient to find a magistrate or the appropriate number of witnesses every time a horse or cow was sold. It would be common in such a sale merely to transfer by *traditio*, even though the buyer would not thereby become owner. We saw in Chapter 4 that the praetors introduced protection for such holders, known as bonitary owners. However, such a holder was not owner according to the civil law. *Usucapio* allowed the situation to be tidied up by giving civil law ownership to the bonitary owner after he had possessed for the necessary time.

The length of time necessary depended on whether the property to be acquired was moveable property or land. Under the Twelve Tables, the required period of possession was 1 year for moveables and 2 years for land. These are remarkably short periods. However, it will be remembered that at the time of the Twelve Tables Rome's power extended only to a limited area of Italy. Such periods may have been adequate in those circumstances, but they were later increased to 3 years for moveables and 10 or 20 years for land, the longer period applying where the owner was domiciled in a different province from the land.

In any case, the possession had to be continuous. If it was interrupted for any reason within the required period, *usucapio* would not operate. The possession would have to start over again. For these purposes, a court action challenging the possessor's right to the property counted as interruption. Thus, if an action was raised, challenging the possession just before the expiry of the time limit, the possessor would not acquire ownership even if he remained in possession until the outcome of the litigation was known. Equally, suppose that the possessor was dispossessed with only a month to go before the completion of the period of *usucapio*. Even if he recovered possession, the previous period of possession would not count. He would need to possess continuously for the full period of *usucapio*.

In addition to possession for the requisite period, there were several other requirements.

The first requirement was *iusta causa*. We saw that this "just cause", a sufficient legal basis for the transfer, was required for the acquisition of ownership by *traditio*. The requirement of *iusta causa* is similar to that for *traditio*. There is one vital difference, however. In *traditio*, we saw that it was enough that the parties believed there to be sufficient *causa*.

Ownership would still pass even if, say, one party thought the transfer was a gift and the other thought it was a sale. For *usucapio*, it was necessary that there be a real *causa*. There must be an actual sale, or gift, or legacy, or whatever the *causa* might be. In other words, *usucapio* operated only where the problem was with the transferor's title or with the mode of transfer used (ie *res mancipi* being transferred by *traditio*).

The second requirement was good faith on the part of the possessor. "Good faith" cannot mean here simply a belief on the part of the possessor in his right to the property, for otherwise the bonitary owner could never acquire by *usucapio*. Such a holder knows that he has taken the property by a method that does not give him ownership. What "good faith" must mean is a belief that one acquired the property from someone with a right to give ownership. Good faith was required only on the taking of possession. Thus, a possessor who discovered the true facts during the period of *usucapio* could still acquire ownership.

The third requirement was that the property was not stolen. This requirement applied only to the acquisition of moveables by *usucapio*, for land could not be stolen. However, in relation to moveables, this requirement imposed a severe restriction on acquisition by *usucapio*. No one could acquire by this method ownership of property that had been stolen. This was the case even if the possessor knew nothing of the theft (the thief would, of course, be barred from *usucapio* anyway, on the basis of being in bad faith). *Usucapio* of moveables was therefore restricted to the limited number of cases where the property found its way into the possession of someone without right to it, without any party involved being aware of the true facts. An example might be property found among the possessions of a deceased person, and assumed by the heir to belong to the deceased. Anyone buying the property could acquire ownership by *usucapio*, even if it transpired that the goods had only been hired by the deceased.

Essential Facts

- There were different ways of acquiring ownership of property. They could be divided into original modes of acquisition and derivative modes of acquisition. In original acquisition, ownership was acquired otherwise than from a previous owner. Derivative acquisition was acquisition from a previous owner.

- *Mancipatio* was a derivative mode of acquisition used for *res mancipi* (see Chapter 4). It involved a ceremonial conveyance before witnesses.
- *In iure cessio* was another derivative mode of acquisition used for *res mancipi*. It required the involvement of a magistrate.
- *Traditio*, or delivery, was the usual mode of acquisition for *res nec mancipi* and, in the later law, for all types of property. Ownership passed when the transferee took possession on a sufficient legal basis for transfer.
- *Occupatio* was an original mode of acquisition, applying to ownerless property, such as wild animals. Ownership was acquired on taking possession of the animal.
- *Specificatio* dealt with the situation where a new thing, called a *nova species*, was made from someone else's materials. If the new thing could not be put back into its original form, Justinian settled the law to the effect that the manufacturer acquired ownership.
- *Accessio* arose when one thing was attached to another. The lesser object was called the "accessory" and the greater the "principal". The accessory became part of the principal, and ownership was acquired by the owner of the principal.
- *Commixtio* and *confusio* were original modes of acquisition that applied when things belonging to more than one person were mixed together. *Commixtio* related to the mixing of solids and *confusio* to the mixing of liquids or gases, but otherwise the doctrines were to the same effect. The owners of the property mixed together shared ownership of the mixture in proportion to their contributions.
- *Usucapio* meant acquisition of ownership by possession for a specified period of time. Different time periods applied to land and to moveable property. At the end of the period of possession, the possessor acquired ownership as long as he took possession in good faith and the property was not stolen.

Essential Cases

Broughton v Aitchison (1809): in a sale of goods, the buyer paid the seller to retain the goods for safekeeping. Even though the seller retained custody, the court held that this was sufficient for delivery, this being therefore an example of *constitutum possessorium*.

Sutter v Aberdeen Arctic Co (1861): the crew of a ship severely injured a whale by harpooning it. The ship then followed the whale. However, before the whale could be taken, the crew from another ship caught and killed it. The court awarded the whale to the crew of the first ship to wound it, as they were pursuing with a reasonable prospect of capture. This represents, therefore, the opposite view of *occupatio* from that of Justinian, who held that actual capture was necessary for the acquisition of ownership.

International Banking Corporation v Ferguson, Shaw & Sons (1909): oil belonging to the pursuers was sold to the defenders by a party who did not own it, and who could not therefore give the defenders any right to it. Unaware that they had acquired no right to the oil, the defenders used it to manufacture lard, which they then sold to various customers. On the basis that *specificatio* had occurred, the court held that the defenders had acquired ownership of the oil but were liable to compensate the pursuers for their loss.

Zahnrad Fabrik Passau GmbH v Terex Ltd (1985): this case concerned the doctrine of *accessio*. It was held that certain axles would have acceded to industrial machinery only if they could not be removed without damage.

6 THE LAW OF THINGS: SUCCESSION

If a person is to be allowed to own property, the law has to have rules for the distribution of that property when the owner dies. A particular legal system may allow a person to make a will, or it may distribute part or all of the deceased's assets according to set rules. Those rules may well be complex, so as to take into account all the eventualities. If wills are allowed, they will also require legal regulation. There is no end to the number of different ways in which a person might decide to distribute his estate, and so the rules for wills are also likely to become complex.

The Roman law of succession, in cases both testate and intestate, was extremely complex. On top of the original *ius civile* rules, there were overlaid layers of praetorian and statutory development. The purpose of this chapter is to give only an overview of the main principles and institutions of the law.

UNIVERSAL SUCCESSION

In modern Scots law, on a person's death his entire estate, consisting of his assets and liabilities, is transferred to another person who is appointed as executor. The executor has the task of paying off the debts and distributing any surplus assets. If there is a will, this distribution will be made in accordance with the intentions of the deceased. However, the executor acts only as a trustee. His role is only that of an administrator of the estate, and he bears no personal liability for the debts of the deceased.

The Roman law followed a very different principle, known as universal succession. In a system of universal succession, the estate of the deceased passes directly to the heir, who is then personally liable for the debts of the deceased, even if they exceed the assets of the estate (the so-called *damnosa hereditas*, or ruinous inheritance). As we shall see, heirs were given various protections, but throughout the development of the Roman law of succession the principle of universal succession remained.

INTESTATE SUCCESSION

There were several stages in the development of the Roman law of intestate succession. However, the original *ius civile* rules, as contained in the Twelve Tables, were not wholly superseded until Justinian. Accordingly, the different stages in the law's development must be understood in the context of the *ius civile* rules.

The *ius civile* rules

In the early law, contained in but probably pre-dating the Twelve Tables, potential heirs were put into different classes, which were arranged in priority. If there was a person entitled to be heir in one class, classes ranked lower were excluded.

The first class of potential heirs consisted of the persons known as *sui heredes*. The term "*sui heredes*" means" "their own heirs" or "heirs to themselves", and were so called because the deceased's property was seen in early law as being in a sense the family's property, of which the *paterfamilias* had merely lifetime stewardship. In this sense, the *sui heredes*, therefore, were seen as having in the property rights of a sort, even before the death of the *paterfamilias*. The *sui heredes* were those who became *sui iuris* on the death of a male deceased (see Chapter 3), in other words the children of the deceased, including adopted children, and also his widow if the marriage was *cum manu*. In the case of a predeceasing son, any child of that son also became *sui iuris* (children of daughters would become *sui iuris* only on the death of their father or his *paterfamilias*) and would represent his or her father in the division of the estate. Children born after the death of their father (*nascituri*) were treated for these purposes as if they had already been born, as is the case in modern Scots law. *Sui heredes* could not refuse to be heirs, even if the estate was insolvent, as they were *necessarii heredes* (see below).

Children who had been emancipated were not *sui heredes*, nor were wives in a marriage *sine manu*, and so such persons had no rights on intestacy.

On a woman's death, her children were not *sui heredes*. The reason for this was that a woman's children were not in her *potestas*, and so did not become *sui iuris* on her death. Thus, this first class of potential heirs was relevant only on a man's death.

If there were no *sui heredes*, the nearest agnatic relation (eg a sibling) would be heir. The question of who was the nearest agnate was answered by counting back to the nearest common ancestor and then back down to the party claiming entitlement. Siblings are thus related in the second degree, uncle and nephew in the third degree and cousins in the fourth. Women were barred in the late Republic from succeeding as agnates, except for sisters of the deceased. The nearest agnate could refuse to be heir, in which case the estate passed to the deceased's *gens* (clan), though this was superseded by developments in the law by the classical period, and the nature of the right of the *gens* is obscure.

Praetorian developments

The praetors intervened extensively in the law of intestacy, which was often seen as neglecting the legitimate claims of more deserving relations. The praetors could not directly change the *ius civile* rules. However, they limited the practical scope of those rules by allowing non-heirs a new remedy – *bonorum possessio* (possession of property) – authorising them to take possession of the estate. *Bonorum possessio* could be granted by the praetor either *cum re* or *sine re*. Where it was granted *cum re*, it was effective even against the *ius civile* heir. Where it was granted *sine re*, however, the *ius civile* heir could recover the property, although he would be subject to the burden of proving his entitlement. The grantee of *bonorum possessio sine re* was therefore in a vulnerable position, although the possession thereby acquired would allow ownership to be obtained by *usucapio* (see Chapter 5).

In strict law, the grantee of *bonorum possessio* was not heir. As a result, at least originally, he could neither enforce any right held by the deceased nor could the deceased's debts be enforced against him. However, by classical law such actions were allowed on the fiction that this "praetorian heir" was the actual heir.

The developed praetorian law prioritised different classes of potential heir. The highest priority was given to children of the deceased, meaning not only any descendant becoming *sui iuris* but also emancipated children. However, where a child had been emancipated, it was necessary to collate any money or property received from the deceased on emancipation (*collatio bonorum*). The value of such money or property would be notionally added to the deceased's estate for the purposes of calculating shares, and would then be deducted from the emancipated child's share.

If the deceased died without issue, the estate would fall to those entitled to be heirs under the *ius civile* rules. Primarily this would mean agnatic relations.

Failing the first two categories of potential heirs in the praetorian system, the nearest cognatic relation (limited to relationships in the sixth degree) would be entitled to be heir. If there were no such relations, a surviving spouse would be entitled to inherit.

Legislation

Further reforms were made by two *senatusconsulta* of the 2nd century AD.

In the *senatusconsultum Tertullianum* of around AD 130, the order of succession was changed where the deceased's mother had had at least three children (four if she was a freedwoman). In such a case, the deceased's issue had first priority. If there were no issue, the deceased's father had priority, followed by any brothers of the whole blood. Failing these categories, the deceased's sisters of the whole blood shared the estate with their mother.

In the *senatusconsultum Orphitianum* of AD 178, the relationship of children to their mother was recognised, and they were given the primary right to succeed on her intestacy, whether they were legitimate or illegitimate.

Neither of these *senatusconsulta* changed the order of succession except in the specific circumstances to which they applied.

Justinian's reforms

Justinian introduced a new scheme, based on relationships of blood (cognatic relationships), without restriction to agnatic relationships.

Highest priority continued to be given to issue of the deceased. Failing this, the estate was divided between ascendants and siblings. If there was no one in those classes, the nearest relation took the estate. If there were no relations, the deceased's spouse took the estate.

TESTATE SUCCESSION

Instead of leaving the distribution of the estate to the rules of intestacy, it was common to make provision for this by means of a will. Indeed, among the upper class, it was seen as irresponsible not to make a will.

Requirements for a valid will

As a starting point, only one who was of sound mind and past the age of puberty could make a will. Usually, the testator also had to be *sui iuris*. We saw in Chapter 3, though, that there were certain instances when property could be owned by persons who were *alieni iuris*. An example of this was the soldier's *peculium castrense*. In such cases, an *alieni iuris* person could make a will.

The will in the developed law had four main characteristics:

"(i) it appoints a universal successor, who may be someone other than the *heres ab intestato* [heir on intestacy]; (ii) it may make gifts (legacies) out of the estate, and may make other particular dispositions (appointment of tutors, manumission of slaves); (iii) it is 'ambulatory', or 'speaks from death' (eg the property disposed of is taken to include things which the testator acquired only after making the will, and a description such as 'my nephews' is taken to include those born since the will was made and to exclude those who have died since then (or rather their heirs)); (iv) it is revocable." (Nicholas, *An Introduction to Roman Law*, pp 252–253)

The Roman will, then, has – in substance if not in form – much in common with the modern will. However, it need not be assumed that the earlier forms of wills in Roman law necessarily had all of these characteristics.

Several types of will were recognised as the law developed. The earliest form of will was the comitial will, which was made before the *comitia curiata*. Less important was the *testamentum in procinctu* ("will made in readiness for battle") which could be made by soldiers before battle.

The comitial will was hardly convenient, however, and both it and the *testamentum in procinctu* became obsolete during the Republic. In the early Republic, a different form of will was developed, known as the mancipatory will. In form, this was a *mancipatio* (see Chapter 5) of the testator's estate in favour of an individual known as *familiae emptor*, who agreed to take the property subject to an obligation to follow the testator's instructions. However, the conveyance and the involvement of the *familiae emptor* as grantee were fictions. The transfer of property occurred only on death, and the recipient was the heir named in the will rather than the *familiae emptor*.

In the later Republic, the practice with mancipatory wills was to record the details of the testator's intentions on wax tablets, sealed by the five witnesses to the *mancipatio* as well as the *familiae emptor* and *libripens*. At this point, the *mancipatio* ceremony itself became essentially superfluous. Accordingly, the praetor allowed enforcement of such wills by *bonorum possessio*, even where the *mancipatio* had not been carried out, as long as the will was sealed by seven witnesses.

Further alterations to the formal requirements of the will were made through the Empire. By Justinian's time, the usual form of will was the "tripartite" will (*testamentum tripertitum*), so called because it was developed from three sources: the *ius civile*, the praetorian law and imperial legislation. The important innovation in this form of will was the requirement for the testator's subscription. In the earlier law, the testator had neither signed nor sealed the will, although the will was protected from forgery by the fact of the witnesses sealing the wax tablets on which it was written. However, wills now tended to be written on sheets of parchment rather than tablets, and so a new method of authentication was necessary.

Appointment of heir

In terms of the content of the will, the only requirement was that it appoint someone as heir. This usually had to be at the beginning of the will, and nothing written before the appointment of the heir was effective if it restricted the heir's rights. The appointment could, however, be conditional. The appointment had to comply with strict requirements of wording, and departure invalidating the will.

It was common to provide for substitutes in case of the failure or refusal of the named heir, in order to prevent the estate falling into intestacy. To provide further security against the failure of the will, the list of substitutes would often include a person falling into the category of persons known as *necessarii heredes*. The *necessarii heredes* were the *sui heredes* together with any slave manumitted by the will. *Necessarii heredes* could not refuse appointment as heir.

Appointment as heir meant, as we have seen, assumption of liability for the deceased's debts. However, steps were taken to protect heirs from the consequences of this. Where the heir was one of the *sui heredes*, the praetor allowed the *ius abstinendi* – the right to abstain. This allowed the deceased's estate to be sold off for the benefit of the creditors, but without any right to recover any shortfall from the heir. To *necessarii heredes* generally there was also allowed the *separatio bonorum* (separation of property), separating the deceased's estate, and therefore the deceased's debts, from anything owed by the deceased to the heir and anything acquired by the heir after the death.

The mixing of the estates of the deceased and the heir also posed risks to the creditors of the deceased, for, while the deceased's estate might be solvent, this might not be the case for the heir's estate. For this reason, the deceased's creditors could also seek the *separatio bonorum*, keeping the deceased's assets separate from those of the heir until the debts were paid.

Restrictions on the contents of wills

There were some restrictions on the contents of wills. As a will was a product of the *ius civile*, only those with Roman citizenship rights could benefit from one. Aside from this, any legacy had to be in favour of an identifiable person and so could not, for example, be in favour of an association of people.

Subject to these points, the Roman testator had almost complete freedom of testation. In addition to the appointment of the heir, the will might include numerous specific legacies, and these would be permissible as long as they were not illegal, immoral or impossible.

To the freedom of testation, however, there were important exceptions in favour of the deceased's family. There was a rule, for example, that *sui heredes* could be disinherited only by express provision in the will. The original justification for this rule was that, as we have seen, the *sui heredes* were in principle entitled to be heirs, and so this entitlement could only be removed by express provision. It should be noted, though, that we are only concerned here with the appointment of heirs. A child who has been excluded from being heir might nonetheless be given a legacy in the will.

By praetorian development, for male *sui heredes*, this disinheritance had to be done by name in the will, although other *sui heredes* could be disinherited as a class. The praetors also extended this rule to the disinheritance of emancipated children, although any money or property previously received by them had to be collated, as with the rules on intestacy considered above.

For the testator who had decided to disinherit his children, however, this restriction merely imposed a technical requirement that was easily overcome. A more important limitation on the freedom of testation was the *querela inofficiosi testamenti* (complaint of an undutiful will), introduced in the late Republic to deal with cases where the testator has unjustly failed to make appropriate provision in the will for his family. This was seen as a breach of family duty. The original basis for this action was that the testator must have been insane in making the will, though this was a fiction – if the testator had really been insane, the will would not have been valid at all.

The *querela* could be brought only by certain classes of person, those being (in order) descendants, ascendants and siblings (though in the last case only if the person instituted as heir was a "base person", such as one who had a disreputable profession). In addition, the *querela* could be brought only by someone who would have been entitled on intestacy, whether under the *ius civile* or through a praetorian remedy.

The rule as it developed was that provision in a will for an individual was regarded as sufficient if it amounted to a quarter of what that person would have received on intestacy, this being known as the *legitima portio*. This idea was received into Scots law as the "legitim" fund, in relation to which the testator is not entitled to test, being a third of the moveable estate if there is a surviving spouse, or a half if not.

The usual effect of a successful challenge under the *querela* was that the will was declared void. This would put the estate into intestacy, although this might be only partial intestacy if not all of a number of heirs were challenged. That this might result from a minor miscalculation in the testator's calculation of the value of his estate, or from a change in the value of the estate following the making of the will, was obviously a practical difficulty. Accordingly, Justinian amended the law. By his amendments, the *querela* was restricted to cases where the party raising the action had been entirely excluded from the will; where provision had been made which was inadequate, he had only an action to make up the deficiency.

Codicils

A codicil was an informal attempt to dispose of property on death, without use of a will. These were first recognised under Augustus. Indeed, the impetus for their recognition was a request made in a codicil, written while its author (one Lentulus), for Augustus himself to carry out a *fideicommissum* (see below). He consulted the leading jurists of the day, who advised him that this was a valid method of proceeding, as it was difficult to comply with the strict requirements for the creation of wills while travelling.

Unlike wills, codicils could be made informally, although the emperor Theodosius II introduced a requirement that there be seven witnesses. This was reduced to five by Justinian. However, the law made a distinction based on whether the codicil was confirmed by a will in proper form, either prospectively or retrospectively. If the will was not so confirmed, it could only validly be used to create a *fideicommissum*.

Fideicommissa

Fideicommissa were first recognised at the same time as codicils, although there was no necessary connection between the two. A *fideicommissum* had similarities to a modern trust, in that it involved property being given to an heir or legatee subject to the condition that the property be used for the benefit of some third party. In origin, the *fideicommissum* was not enforceable. The name merely refers to something that has been "committed to the faith" of a person. However, enforcement of *fideicommissa* was permitted from the reign of Augustus onwards.

The *fideicommissum* was an extremely flexible institution, allowing the evasion of many of the usual rules of succession. Thus, for example, we have seen that a foreigner was not allowed to benefit from a Roman will. Such a person could, though, be the beneficiary of a *fideicommissum*. Accordingly, one wanting to make a legacy to a foreigner would simply avoid the prohibition by making a *fideicommissum* in his favour.

A very important use of *fideicommissa* was for attempts to keep property within families. Because a *fideicommissum* could be used to impose *fideicommissa* on persons not yet alive (called "fideicommissary substitution"), property could be handed down through the family, with each successive heir being bound to pass it on to his eldest son. Such arrangements in favour of "uncertain persons" were prohibited by the emperor Hadrian in the 2nd century AD, although allowed again by Justinian, and the number of generations for which similar arrangements could endure was restricted.

Essential Facts

- Roman law operated a system of universal succession. In this system, the heir of a deceased person was liable for the deceased's debts.
- For intestate succession, the Twelve Tables imposed a system based on agnatic relationships, where the *sui heredes*, ie those becoming *sui iuris* on the death of the deceased, were the persons primarily entitled to be heirs.
- This system was modified by praetorian intervention recognising the claims of emancipated children and cognatic relations.
- The main requirement for a valid will was the appointment of an heir. The will might also contain specific legacies to individual legatees.
- The testator had, for the most part, unlimited powers of testation. However, this was limited by the need to disinherit *sui heredes* expressly, and more importantly by the right given to those who would be entitled on intestacy to challenge the will as an *inofficiosum testamentum*.

Essential Cases

Douglas v Douglas (1876): a father left his whole estate to one of his two sons, excluding the other on the basis that adequate provision had previously been made for him through lifetime advances. The excluded son made a claim on the legitim fund. It was held, on the basis of the Roman principle of *collatio bonorum*, that the lifetime advances had to be collated. The result in this case was that the excluded son was entitled to nothing from the legitim fund.

7 THE LAW OF THINGS: CONTRACTS

THE LAW OF OBLIGATIONS

Having considered the law of property and the law of succession, we now move on to the other part of the law of things, namely the law of obligations. Whereas property law is the law of real rights, the law of obligations is the law of personal rights. The law of obligations is further subdivided, and in this chapter we look at the first of these subdivisions: obligations arising from contract. However, it is necessary first to examine what is meant by the term "obligation" itself.

An obligation is "a legal tie which binds us to the necessity of making some performance in accordance with the laws of our state" (J.3.13pr). In other words, this is a personal right – a "tie" between two people, not affecting third parties. Thus, where (for example) two parties enter into a contract, no third party has any obligations in relation to that contract. Suppose that A agrees to sell an item of property to B. Instead of completing the sale by delivering the property to B, A instead delivers it to C under a subsequent contract of sale. C becomes owner, and is not affected by the previous agreement with B.

Obligations can be classified in various ways. Gaius divided obligations into two categories: those arising from contracts and those arising from delicts (civil wrongs). However, this fails to take into account a number of types of obligation falling into neither category. Justinian adds to these categories two additional ones: obligations arising "as if" from a contract (*quasi ex contractu*) and those arising "as if" from a delict (*quasi ex delicto*). These categories take in various types of obligation arising neither from contract nor from delict but having some feature in common with either contracts or delicts. These additional categories of obligation are considered in Chapter 9. Delicts are considered in Chapter 8.

TRANSFER OF OBLIGATIONS

We have seen that the law of obligations is part of the law of things. If, then, an obligation is to be seen as a form of property, one might think that it would be possible for the creditor to transfer the right to performance to someone else. Such transfers are very common in the modern law, and go by the name of "assignation". In assignation, the original creditor (or assignor) transfers his rights to the new creditor (or assignee).

It does not appear, however, that assignation was permitted in early or classical Roman law. The "legal tie" of the obligation was seen as binding the two parties to each other personally. One reason for this might perhaps be that enforcement of the obligation might be against the debtor's person, rather than his property, through enslavement (see Chapter 10). It might have been thought unfair potentially to substitute a lenient creditor, with whom the debtor chose to contract, with a harsh creditor.

Commerce, however, demands that the value of a person's assets be realisable, and there are many instances in which it would be desirable to transfer the right to performance of an obligation. One device that was used to avoid the non-recognition of assignation was novation (ie a new obligation being substituted for the old), with a new creditor being substituted for the old creditor. However, as this was a new obligation, the involvement of the debtor would be required.

An alternative was to enter into an arrangement with the "assignee" whereby he was authorised to sue the debtor in his own name and keep what he received. This arrangement was known as *procuratio in rem suam*. However, it had the disadvantage that the "assignor" remained in law the creditor and could revoke the authority of the "assignee" at any time before the case had passed from the consideration of the praetor.

As the law developed, steps were taken to protect the situation of the "assignee" in a *procuratio in rem suam*. The process was completed by the time of Justinian, and an action was given to an assignee to enforce the obligation if it was clear that the parties had intended to transfer the right to enforcement. The assignee was then able to sue in his own right.

TERMINATION OF OBLIGATIONS

An obligation could come to an end in various ways.

The most obvious way in which an obligation is extinguished is by performance. Once a person pays a debt he owes, or performs some action that he is required to perform, he is freed from the obligation. This will also be the outcome if someone else performs on the debtor's behalf.

Sometimes a creditor will find it convenient to accept some alternative performance in place of what is actually owed. If, for example, it is impossible for the specific goods agreed under a contract of sale to be supplied, the buyer might agree to accept equivalent goods. Alternatively, different terms for the obligation might be agreed, this being called "novation" as it constitutes a new obligation. Thus, for instance, a creditor might accept payment in instalments rather than in the agreed lump sum if the debtor is having difficulty making payment. As we have seen, it was also possible to substitute new parties into the agreement.

Again, a creditor might waive performance of the obligation altogether. This is called acceptilation. For example, as we shall see in Chapter 8, if A negligently injures B, that gave rise to an obligation on the part of A to compensate B for his loss. However, it was always open to B not to insist on this, and if he absolved A of the obligation to pay, the obligation would be extinguished. Justinian tells us that acceptilation was available only for *stipulationes* (see below). However, the obligation could be converted to a *stipulatio*, and then acceptilated.

We can see then that the law allowed an obliged party only two options: either he performed the obligation or he obtained his creditor's consent to his release from the obligation. In the absence of such consent, the party under the obligation was subject to an absolute requirement to comply with it.

THE LAW OF CONTRACTS

Roman law did not have a general law of contract. For a contract to be enforceable, it had to fall within one of the types specified by the law. This contrasts with modern law, in which any seriously intended agreement is in principle enforceable: as Stair says for Scots law, "every paction produceth action" (Stair, *Institutions* 1,10,7). A modern textbook on contract law will be mostly made up of consideration of general principles, with specific types of contract (such as sale or hire) being considered separately or not at all. For the Romans, the priority is reversed. In the Roman sources, the emphasis is on the specific contracts, with barely any recognition of common principles applying to contracts generally.

The Institutional Scheme divided contracts into four categories, depending on how they were constituted. These are:

(1) obligations arising by conduct;

(2) obligations arising by words;

(3) obligations arising by writing; and

(4) obligations arising by agreement.

It will be seen, therefore, that it is not enough that there is an agreement. The parties must also comply with the specific requirements for the contract in question before a valid contract can be said to have been constituted.

OBLIGATIONS ARISING BY CONDUCT

Four types of contract are identified by Justinian as arising by conduct. In each case, the conduct in question is the delivery of an item of property.

Mutuum

The contract of *mutuum* was one of the two contracts of loan, the other being *commodatum*. How these differ is that *mutuum* applies to generic goods identified as so much of a particular thing measured by weight, quantity or other measure. What the borrower is to return is the equivalent, not the same property he borrowed. Typically, the object of a contract of *mutuum* would be something consumed by use, such as food, drink or money. In *commodatum*, on the other hand, what the borrower is to return to the lender is the very thing lent. In both cases, the contract was constituted by the delivery of the property borrowed to the borrower.

It might be thought from the inclusion of loans of money under the heading of *mutuum* that this contract would have been of considerable commercial importance. However, its importance in this regard was restricted by the fact that it was gratuitous, although provision for payment of interest could be made by *stipulatio* (see below).

In *mutuum*, ownership of the property passed to the borrower. For this reason, the borrower was liable to make repayment even if the property was destroyed.

Commodatum

Commodatum was a loan for use. Unlike in the case of *mutuum*, the borrower in a contract of *commodatum* did not acquire ownership of the property and was under an obligation to return the same item to the lender. The borrower was not liable for accidental damage to the property, although he was obliged to take care of the property and would be liable in the case of any damage caused by his fault.

As with *mutuum*, *commodatum* was gratuitous. If any charge was made, the contract would be one of hire.

Deposit

The contract of deposit involved property being handed over to a person called a depositee, to be looked after. The depositee had no entitlement to use the property, or the appropriate contract would be *commodatum*. The depositee was liable to return the property, but was liable only for damage he had caused intentionally. The depositee was not even liable if he negligently damaged the property.

Pledge

The fourth contract falling into this category was the contract of pledge. The delivery of an item of property to a creditor in security for a debt gave the creditor a real right in that property, and we have already looked at pledge in that context (see Chapter 4).

OBLIGATIONS ARISING BY WORDS

The category of obligations arising by words was an old one, existing already by the time of the Twelve Tables. The main example was the contract called *stipulatio*.

A *stipulatio* was constituted by a formal exchange of words, whereby one party, the promisor, would promise to perform some action. What was required was for the promisee to ask the promisor whether he promised to perform the action. This would be done by asking a question in the form *"spondesne ...?"* ("Do you promise ...?"), to which the reply would be *"spondeo"* ("I promise"). As the formation of the contract was dependent on spoken words, the parties had to be present. Originally, the words given here, *"spondesne"* and *"spondeo"*, had to be used or there would be no valid *stipulatio*. Even other words with the same meaning were not sufficient. However, through time, this requirement was relaxed and other words and other languages were permitted. The question and answer also had to follow the form given here. The answer was a simple acceptance of what was contained in the question, and so could not introduce conditions. Any condition would have to be included in the question, which could therefore be quite complex.

What is notable about *stipulatio* as compared with other forms of contract is its possible content. While the other recognised contracts dealt with specific types of transaction, a *stipulatio* could relate to any type of transaction that was not illegal, impossible or immoral. *Stipulationes* were therefore used in a wide variety of contexts. We have already seen that they could be used for novation, but there were many other possibilities.

The wide scope of the contract of *stipulatio* raises the question of its potential to form the basis of a general law of contract. It is not clear to what extent this was achieved by Justinian's time, although there was certainly movement in that direction. In practice, the agreement would often be recorded in writing, that writing taking for practical purposes the place of the spoken agreement. It might be said, therefore, that there was a general law of contract so far as written contracts were concerned. In relation to oral contracts, however, the formality of the *stipulatio* would hamper developments of that type.

OBLIGATIONS CREATED BY WRITING

This category refers to an old form of constitution of obligation by means of an entry in a household account book acknowledging a debt. The obligation thus created was dependent on the account entry, not on any valid underlying agreement. This category of contract was probably obsolete even by Gaius's day.

Although by his time this form of contract was long obsolete, it is included by Justinian in the *Institutes*. However, on examination it would appear that he is talking about something else – about the difficulties of disproving the validity of an obligation that has been constituted in writing. Time limits applied to any such attempt, beyond which the obligation's validity was not in dispute. However, the assumption is that there is some other form of contract underlying the written acknowledgement.

OBLIGATIONS ARISING BY AGREEMENT

Four contracts are classified as arising by agreement: sale, hire, partnership and mandate. For these contracts, no formalities are required beyond the presence of agreement.

Sale

Requirements of the contract of sale

A sale was the exchange of ownership of property for money. The contract was concluded when these two essential elements – subject-matter – and price, were agreed on. This was the case even where payment of the price or delivery of the goods was to take place at a later date.

The general rule was that the price had to be certain. Justinian, however, laid down that if the price was to be fixed by a third party this was to be a valid contract of sale, conditional on the price being fixed. There was in the classical law some dispute between the Sabinians and the Proculians as to whether the price had to be in money, or whether payment could be in the form of goods. The view eventually taken, however, was that the price had to be a monetary one. The price had to be a real price, so if the seller did not intend to take the agreed payment, the contract was void. Finally, there was some control over the fairness of pricing. In the case of a contract for sale of land, the seller could rescind the contract where the price was less than half of the land's value. This situation, of a grossly unfair price, was known as *laesio enormis*.

As noted, it was also necessary to agree the subject-matter of the contract. The subject-matter had to be an existing thing, so the contract was void if the thing had never existed or had perished at the time of making the contract. There was, however, apparently exception for future crops and offspring of live property.

It was not necessary for the seller to be the owner of the property. If a person contracted to sell property he had no right to sell, that was nonetheless a valid contract of sale. The buyer's interest in such a case was protected by the seller's obligation of warrandice, considered below.

Error

The general principle was that if the parties were not agreed on the subject-matter or the price, the contract was void for lack of agreement. Thus, if one thing was sold for another, as, for example, where A intended to sell one field but B intended to buy another, there was no contract. Greater difficulty was found where the parties had agreed on the thing to be sold but differed as to its nature or qualities. To meet this, the doctrine of *error in substantia* (error in the substantials) developed. Where the parties were in error with regard to the fundamental characteristics of the property, the contract was void. Various examples are given in the sources, such as vinegar sold as wine; gold or lead sold as silver; or a slave of one sex sold as the other. It was not, however, every error that would have this effect. Lesser errors would not render a contract void. One example given of such a lesser error was the virginity or otherwise of a slave. It is not always easy to distinguish errors *in substantia* from other errors, though. For example, although we are told that it is such an error where one metal is sold for another, we are also told that it is not such an error where an alloy is sold as a pure metal. It is not easy to devise a principle that adequately explains this distinction.

Risk

What happens if the property is damaged or destroyed before delivery to the buyer? Is the buyer still required to pay? The relevant concept here is "risk". The rule was that risk passed on completion of the contract, even though (because of the requirement for delivery) the seller was still the owner. Thus, if the property was destroyed or damaged after the contract was made, the buyer would nonetheless be bound to pay the agreed price. This is also the rule in modern Scots law for sales of land, though the position has been changed with regard to sales of moveable property.

The seller's obligations

The seller was obliged to give the buyer peaceable possession of the property. If the buyer was evicted, the seller would be liable for this. This obligation is known as warrandice. "Eviction" in this context means the establishment of a better right to the property by someone else, rather than physical ejection. Note that this was only a guarantee against eviction, not a guarantee of ownership. If it transpired that the seller did not own the property, the buyer nonetheless had no remedy for this unless and until the actual owner evicted him by making a claim to the property. This is also the rule in modern Scots law for sales of land. The position has been changed in the modern law with regard to sales of moveable property.

Originally, the seller bore no liability for any defects in the goods. In the late Republic, however, the jurists developed a ground of liability where the seller knew of the defect. Latent defects were not covered though. The aediles' edict introduced a remedy for defects in slaves and cattle sold in the marketplace. Where there was such a defect, the buyer could rescind the contract if the defect was material. Alternatively, if the defect was not material, the seller could claim the difference in value caused by the defect by means of an action called the *actio quanti minoris*. By the time of Justinian, this had been expanded to being the rule for all contracts of sale.

Hire

The Roman texts identify a contract called hire. They do not, however, distinguish expressly between different forms of this contract. This is the case even though it is apparent that under this head fall several distinct types of relationship. Modern works on Roman law distinguish three types of hire:

(1) the hire of property: this includes both land and moveable property;

(2) hire of a piece of work, as where a tradesman is engaged to manufacture some item;

(3) hire of services: this can be distinguished from the hire of a piece of work on the basis of being an ongoing relationship, more like a contract of employment. The hire of services was restricted to low-status occupations, of the type usually done by slaves.

Hire was governed by rules in some respects similar to those applying to sale. There had to be a price in money and the parties had to be agreed on the subject-matter of the contract.

Distinguishing hire and sale

It was sometimes difficult to distinguish hire from sale. For example, where land was to be enjoyed by the "hirer" in perpetuity as long as rent continued to be paid, this was in substance very similar to a sale. The emperor Zeno in the 5th century AD established this as a separate institution called *emphyteusis*.

Another example where there might be difficulty was the contract providing for the manufacture of something by one of the parties. An example of this would be a goldsmith engaged to make rings. The rule for cases of this kind was that, if the smith used his own gold, the contract was sale. If the customer supplied the gold, the contract was one of hire.

The parties' obligations

The hirer had to comply with the express terms of the hire. In the absence of express agreement, a hirer of property had to keep it "as carefully as the most careful owner would keep his own property" (J.3.24.5). The hirer would be liable for any damage caused by his fault, but the owner would have to bear any loss resulting from ordinary wear and tear or accidental damage.

In a hire of services or a hire of a piece of work, either party was liable for any loss caused to the other by his fault.

In a hire of work, the party making the order bore the risk of damage by act of God or caused by defect in materials supplied by him. Otherwise, the risk was borne by the party carrying out work.

Partnership

Partnership was an arrangement whereby two or more parties pooled property or labour. Unlike the modern partnership, this was not necessarily a commercial relationship. Partnership could cover all the partners' assets or only a single line of business or a particular transaction.

In the absence of agreement between the partners, profits and losses from the partnership were shared equally.

Each partner was expected to show in relation to the partnership affairs "the same care as he usually displays in his own" (J.3.25.9). The partners were liable to each other for any loss caused by their failure to meet this standard.

Partnership was brought to an end by renunciation by any of the partners or by the death of any partner, unless the contrary was agreed when the partnership was established. Where the partnership was entered into for a specific matter, it ended when that matter was dealt with. Partnership was also ended if one of the partners was subject to bankruptcy proceedings.

How were the assets of the partnership divided on dissolution? Justinian considers this question:

> "if someone is sharp to withdraw with an eye to a profit for himself, for example where a partner in all worldly wealth is left heir to somebody's estate and renounces the partnership in order to take the inheritance himself, he will be compelled to share his profit." (J.3.25.4)

However, where there was no such intention, he could keep the gain for himself. Subject to this exception, the partners could keep any property acquired after dissolution.

Mandate

Mandate involved one person (the mandatary) acting on behalf of another (the mandator). This contract arose only where the mandatary was to act at least partly on another's behalf, although Justinian points out that one can be acting partly for one's own benefit as well for the benefit of another. It was essential to the contract of mandate that the mandatary be acting gratuitously, and mandate can be distinguished from the modern law of agency on this ground.

The mandatary was not to exceed the limits of the mandate. However, there was a dispute between the Sabinians and the Proculians over the result of exceeding the mandate. Suppose, for example, that the mandatary had a mandate to buy a particular thing for 100, but in fact paid more. The Sabinians said that the mandatary could recover nothing. The Proculians, however, took the view that the mandatary should be entitled to recover 100 from the mandator, though he would be left to bear the excess himself. The latter view was ultimately settled as the correct view.

The mandate could be revoked by the mandator or mandatary at any time before there was a change of position on the part of either party. However, if the mandatary withdrew he was expected to notify the mandator promptly. Unless he had good reason for not doing so, the mandatary would be liable for any prejudice caused to the mandator by this failure. The mandate was ended immediately by the death of either party, although the mandatary would still be entitled to raise an action on the mandate to recover his expenses in complying with the mandate if he carried through the commission in ignorance of the mandator's death.

INNOMINATE CONTRACTS AND PACTS

The categories of contract noted above could not cover every situation where two parties entered into an agreement with the intention that it should be legally enforceable. For this reason, as the law developed other forms of agreement were given some legal recognition.

The first category of such agreements was that of innominate contracts. These contracts were bilateral (ie they imposed obligations on both parties) and involved an agreement to pay, give or do something. Examples include barter (*permutatio*) and agreements where goods were supplied on the basis that either an agreed price would be paid or the goods would be returned (*aestimatum*). The praetor would allow the enforcement of an innominate contract in the situation where one party had performed his side of the bargain and the other had not.

Pacts were agreements that did not fall either within the recognised categories of contracts or within the category of innominate contracts. These were not normally directly enforceable, but could be pled as a defence to an action. Some pacts were, however, made directly enforceable by praetorian or imperial intervention. Examples included *constitutum* (an agreement to pay a debt) and *receptum* (an agreement by a shipowner, innkeeper or stablekeeper to keep safe goods entrusted to him).

Essential Facts

- The law of obligations is concerned with personal rights, rather than real rights.
- The Institutional Scheme distinguishes between contracts, delicts and a number of other types of obligation, called by Justinian "quasi-delict" and "quasi-contract".

- Roman law had no general law of contract. Instead, specific contracts were recognised, divided into four categories in the Institutional Scheme. The recognised categories were contracts created by conduct; contracts created by words; contracts created by writing; and contracts created by agreement.

- The contracts created by conduct all involved the delivery of some item of property. These were the two contracts of loan (*mutuum* and *commodatum*), deposit and pledge. All except pledge were gratuitous.

- The main form of contract created by words was *stipulatio*, which was created by a formal exchange of words. Unlike the other contracts, it was not restricted as to content.

- The contract created by writing was an old form of contract created by entering a debt in an account book.

- The contract of sale was one of the contracts created by agreement. It required the exchange of a price in money for delivery of the property. The seller did not, however, guarantee ownership – only that the buyer would not be evicted from possession of the property.

- Hire, though identified in the Roman sources as a single contract, was in fact three related types of contract created by agreement. The three types of hire were hire of a thing; hire of services; and hire of a piece of work. In all cases, it was necessary to agree on the subject-matter and hire charge.

- Partnership was a contract created by agreement, which involved two or more parties pooling resources or labour. Unlike a modern partnership, this was not necessarily a commercial arrangement.

- Mandate was a contract created by agreement, and involved one person being commissioned to act gratuitously on behalf of another.

Essential Cases

Sloans Dairies Ltd v Glasgow Corporation (1977): the parties entered into a contract for the sale of certain buildings. Before ownership was transferred, the buildings were seriously damaged by fire. The court held that the Roman rule applied: that risk passed on the making of the contract. Accordingly, the buyers were obliged to pay notwithstanding the damage.

Duncan v The MFV Marigold Pd145 (2006): Roman authority (Paul, D.3.5.21) on the conduct of the winding-up of a partnership following the death of a partner was discussed in relation to the same issue in modern law.

Marjandi Ltd v Bon Accord Glass Ltd (2007): this case contains extensive discussion of the classification of contracts of hire drawn from the French *ius commune* writer Pothier, himself referring to J.3.24.4.

8 THE LAW OF THINGS: DELICTS

In the last chapter we looked at the first part of the law of obligations, the law of contracts. In this chapter we move on to the next type of obligation: delicts. A delict is a civil wrong (the word has the same root as "delinquent").

We saw in Chapter 7 that the Romans did not have a single law of contract, instead having a number of recognised contracts. Unless the praetor or the emperor could be persuaded to recognise liability in a new situation, it would be necessary to show that an agreement fitted into one of the established contracts. There was no general principle, as there is in modern law, that seriously intended agreements were enforceable. This is why we speak of Roman law as having a "law of contracts" rather than a "law of contract".

The same is true in the case of delictual liability. Justinian tells us that delictual liability arises "from wrongdoing" (J.4.1pr). But he then tells us that liability arises under one of four heads: "theft, robbery, loss wrongfully caused, or contempt". In addition to these, a number of other types of wrong, known as "praetorian delicts", were also recognised.

One other point that is noteworthy about Roman delicts is that often penal damages were payable. This contrasts with the modern law of delict, where damages are strictly compensatory. The aim in the modern law is, so far as possible, to put the pursuer back in the position he would have been in but for the defender's actions. Any punishment for the defender's actions is a matter for the public authorities. In early legal systems, however, without developed criminal prosecution authorities, the law of delicts takes on this function of punishment and deterrence. Roman law is typical of this.

THEFT (*FURTUM*) AND ROBBERY (*RAPINA*)

We are concerned here with theft and robbery as matters of private law, rather than of criminal law. Theft is defined by Justinian as "the handling of a thing with fraudulent intention" (J.4.1.1), "thing" in this context meaning moveable property. The jurist Paul adds the requirement that the handling take place "with a view to gain" (D.47.2.1.3), although in the typical case this could be assumed from the fact of the appropriation of the goods. There is thus both a physical and a mental element: the physical handling of the goods, and the mental intention to gain from the handling.

In early law, it would appear that there was a requirement that the goods were actually carried off. However, in the developed law, as we see from Justinian's definition, all that was required in terms of the physical element was "handling" of the goods. This meant that removal was not required, although of course removal would make the intention to commit theft easier to prove. Matters of proof aside, though, the physical requirements for theft were satisfied wherever there was handling of goods by a person without consent. This included the case where a person, with custody of goods with the consent of the owner, made unauthorised use. Thus, a depositee or a creditor holding goods on pledge committed theft if he used the goods. A borrower under a contract of *commodatum* (see Chapter 7) committed theft if he used the thing borrowed for a purpose other than that for which it was lent. This would not be the case with a borrower under a contract of *mutuum*, however, as such a borrower became the owner of the goods.

One could be liable for theft without actual handling of the goods if one assisted another in committing a theft. Thus, where A knocked coins from B's hand so that C could steal them, or where A gave B a ladder to break into C's house, A would be jointly liable with the actual thief. This was the case, though, only where there was actual assistance, and this was aimed at the commission of a theft.

The handling of the goods constituted theft only if it was done with a fraudulent intention. In the case of theft by handling, it was necessary to know that the owner did not or would not consent to the use being exercised. The owner himself could be guilty of theft if the goods were in the custody of someone entitled to retain the property. An example of this would be a debtor taking property held by a creditor under pledge. In such a case, the creditor could competently sue the debtor for theft, even though the debtor was owner.

There were also some other occasions where a non-owner could competently sue for theft. Where the property was held by anyone with a financial interest in the property, that person had an action for theft against anyone committing theft of the goods. Indeed, in the case of property held by someone under a contract of hire of work (eg a tailor or a laundryman), Justinian (J.4.1.15) even denies action of theft to the owner. The reason for this is that the owner "has no interest in the safety of the clothes, since he can recover from the laundryman or the tailor in the action on hire". The action was not, though, extended to those with no financial interest in the property. Thus, a depositee had no action for theft as the depositee was only liable to the owner for his own deliberate misconduct.

A distinction was made between manifest and non-manifest theft. Manifest theft was committed where the thief "is seen or caught with the stolen thing, in public or private, by the owner or anyone else, before he reaches the place where he planned to stow it" (J.4.1.3). For manifest theft, damages of four times value of property were payable to the victim. Only double damages were payable for non-manifest theft. In both cases, of course, this represents penal damages.

Robbery was a related delict, introduced by the praetor in the 1st century BC. It was an aggravated form of theft, distinguished by the use of force. The action for robbery gave a remedy of fourfold damages if it was brought within a year of the robbery.

INIURIA

The action for *iniuria*, which can be translated as contempt or insult, lay for insulting behaviour of all kinds. This was a wide-ranging delict, covering, for example, assault, "vocal attack" (*convicium*), defamatory writings, seizure of the victim's goods as if he was an insolvent debtor, and what would in modern terms be considered stalking or sexual harassment. The central idea was that the behaviour complained of constituted an affront to the victim's honour. For this reason, one might also have an action for insults to one's family members. For example, where a woman was the victim of an *iniuria*, in addition to her own action her husband and *paterfamilias* also had an action. A wife was not, however, considered to suffer *iniuria* when her husband was insulted. A slave could not suffer *iniuria* but the master could be insulted through the slave. This would only be the case, though, with serious conduct, "manifestly in contempt of the owner" (J.4.4.3). Thus, flogging another's slave was *iniuria* to the master but the case where "someone abuses a slave vocally or strikes him with a fist" (J.4.4.3) would not be.

An action for *iniuria* could also arise where the insulting behaviour complained of was directed at a deceased person. The action would lie in favour of the heir of the deceased:

"And if, as it happens, *iniuria* is inflicted on the corpse of a dead person from whom we have inherited or received possession of the estate, we have the action on *iniuria* in our own name; for it concerns our reputation if *iniuria* is inflicted on the corpse. Likewise also if the reputation is attacked of a person from whom we have inherited." (Ulpian, D.47.10.1.4)

Liability did not arise unless the insult was unjustifiable. The law did not protect against justifiable insults. Thus, if it could be shown that a defamatory statement was true, no action would lie.

There had to be an intention to insult. Where the insulting behaviour occurred accidentally, or even negligently, no liability arose. Thus, if A accidentally or carelessly knocked B over, B would not be considered to have suffered *iniuria*. If A had done this intentionally, however, he would be liable, assuming that the other requirements for the delict were met. Equally, if A struck B as a joke or during a wrestling match, there would be no liability for *iniuria*. Again, in the example given earlier of a person's goods seized as if he were a debtor, one who initiated such a process believing a debt to be due would not be guilty of *iniuria*. Such a person would be liable only if he knew that there was nothing owing.

The final requirement was that the victim must have suffered upset. If the victim let the insult pass, he could not subsequently change his mind and revive the insult. In practical terms, therefore, the action for *iniuria* would have to be raised as soon after the insult as was reasonably practicable.

THE *LEX AQUILIA*

The *lex Aquilia* was enacted by the plebeian assembly (see Chapter 2) during the Republic, with a traditional date of 287 BC. The first and third of its three sections, or "chapters", imposed delictual liability in certain circumstances. For a long time, the content of the second section was lost, and was the subject of much scholarly debate. However, the rediscovery of Gaius's *Institutes* revealed that the second section was concerned with liability of an entirely different type, long since obsolete by Justinian's time: the liability of an adstipulator (a person appointed by the promisee in a *stipulatio* to recover what was owed by the promisor) who wrongfully discharged the debt. We are not concerned with the second section here.

The basis of liability under the first and third sections of the *lex Aquilia* was *damnum iniuria datum* (loss caused by wrongful conduct). Thus, liability arose where:

(i)   a party had suffered loss, which had been

(ii) caused by

(iii) another's wrongful act.

If these criteria were met, liability was established, provided that the loss that had arisen fell within the terms of the legislation. The starting point, then, is the wording of the *lex Aquilia* itself. It should be noted, however, that juristic interpretation extended the scope of the *lex* beyond its original scope. The praetors also extended the scope of Aquilian liability, by being prepared to grant an action in appropriate circumstances, by analogy with Aquilian liability, called an *actio utilis* or *actio in factum*.

After considering the terms of the first and third sections, we shall look at the general requirements for establishing liability under the *lex Aquilia*, namely loss, fault and causation.

The first section

According to Gaius, the first section of the *lex Aquilia* ran as follows:

> "If anyone kills unlawfully a slave or servant-girl belonging to someone else or a four-footed beast of the class of cattle, let him be condemned to pay the owner the highest value that the property had attained in the preceding year." (D.9.2.2pr)

The first section is therefore concerned with the killing of slaves and livestock, and not with any other type of damage or any other type of property. The types of animal covered by the section are those that graze. Thus, sheep or cows are included, but not dogs or wild animals. The category of grazing animals is taken to include pigs. Justinian justifies this (at J.4.3.1) by reference to the Greek poet Homer, who refers in his *Odyssey* to pigs grazing.

The killing of the animal or slave fell within the section if there was deliberate violence, but also in any other case where death resulted from fault. Thus, if A carelessly slipped and fell, crushing slave B to death, that would fall within the first section.

It will be noted here that there is potentially a penal aspect in any action under the first section. The measure of damages is the highest value the slave or animal had in the previous year, even if it subsequently lost value. Thus, if, for example, a slave had lost a limb within the previous year, damages for the slave's death would nonetheless be based on the value the slave had had before the loss of the limb. The damages payable could thus be considerably higher than the actual loss resulting from the offending party's fault.

The third section

The third section is concerned with cases where the damage caused or the type of property concerned does not fall within the first section.

Thus, non-fatal injuries to slaves or livestock, or damage to other types of property, would be considered under this section. Ulpian reports the terms of the third section as follows:

> "In the case of all other things apart from slaves or cattle that have been killed, if anyone does damage to another by wrongfully burning, breaking or rending his property, let him be condemned to pay to the owner whatever the damage shall prove to be worth in the next 30 days." (D.9.2.27.5).

As a preliminary point, it should be noted that it cannot be said with complete confidence that this reflects what the third section said. It is sometimes said that the damages are to be measured according to the maximum value the property had in the previous 30 days, not according to the diminution in value measured at the end of 30 days. It is also unclear whether it is only the owner's loss for which the wrongdoer is liable, or whether he had to pay the full value of the property. The latter would not be unreasonable if the damage was as serious as is suggested by the words "burning, breaking or rending". However, the type of damage covered was in fact broader than this:

> "...For if anything is burned or rent or broken, an action is established by this chapter; but the term 'rent' could suffice for all these cases. For a thing is construed as 'rent' (*ruptum*) when it is 'spoiled' (*corruptum*) in any way. Hence this word includes not only things burned or rent or broken, but also things torn and dashed and poured out and in any way harmed or destroyed and so diminished in value." (Gaius, G.3.217)

Thus, in the classical law, any type of damage to property was covered by the *lex Aquilia*. This might be the case even where the property was not actually physically harmed but where the owner was deprived of its use. One example given in the texts is of wine poured out. The wine is thereby lost, and liability under the *lex Aquilia* established, without necessarily any physical damage. Another example was where A knocked coins from B's hand, with the result that they fell into a river or down a sewer. Although the coins are physically unharmed, A is in this example deprived of their use and has an action under the *lex Aquilia*.

Loss

The first of the three requirements for liability under the *lex Aquilia* was that loss had to be shown. Even if there had been wrongful conduct, there was no liability if this had not in fact caused loss. Thus, suppose that a slave has been injured. If the slave's value was reduced by the injury, this requirement would be satisfied. Again, if the slave was unable, on account of the injury, to perform his usual duties, the person who wrongfully caused the injury would be liable. However, if the injury was one from which there were no such adverse consequences to the master, there would be no liability under the *lex Aquilia*.

The measure of damages would depend on which section of the *lex Aquilia* applied to the case, as we saw above. By juristic interpretation, the damages would also include any consequential loss. An example of such loss is the case where one of a team of horses was killed, or a slave who was one of a troupe of actors died. The damages payable would take into account the reduction in value of the surviving horses or actors resulting from the loss of one of the team. Again, a slave might be appointed heir to a person who then died. When the slave accepted the estate, it would pass to the master. However, if the slave was killed before accepting the estate, the benefit to the master would be lost. This loss would be counted towards the amount payable in the action under the *lex Aquilia*.

Wrongful conduct

Pure omissions did not give rise to any liability. The possibility of an action under the *lex Aquilia* usually only arose if loss had been caused by some positive action. However, even if a person's actions caused loss, there was no liability under the *lex Aquilia* if there was no *culpa* (fault). Purely accidental injuries did not give rise to any liability:

> "While several persons were playing ball, one of them pushed a slave boy when he tried to catch the ball; the slave fell and broke his leg. Question was raised whether the slave boy's owner can bring suit under the *lex Aquilia* against the person through whose push he fell. I responded that this is not possible, since the event is held to have occurred more by accident than by *culpa*." (Alfenus, D.9.2.52.4)

The Roman texts do not, however, disclose a single, clear test of what is meant by fault, nor did they have any developed concept of contributory negligence, whereby responsibility for the injury is divided between the wrongdoer and the injured party. Characteristically, the jurists proceeded on a case-by-case basis to determine who, in the circumstances, could be said to be responsible for the loss:

> "But if, when persons were throwing javelins in sport, a slave was killed, the Aquilian action lies. However if, while others were throwing javelins in a

field, the slave crossed through this area, the Aquilian action fails, since he ought not to have passed inopportunely through a field reserved for javelin-throwing." (Ulpian, D.9.2.9.4)

In some cases, the question of fault appears to depend at least partially on whether there was a legal right to perform the actions complained of, or whether the injured party had any right to be where he was. Thus, where a slave was injured by a javelin, there would be liability if the javelin was thrown by a soldier in a practice field, but anyone else using the practice field would be liable, as would a soldier throwing a javelin elsewhere. Again, where a person pruning a tree threw down branches, there would be no liability where the injured party was on private land where he had no right to be. If the tree was next to a public road, on the other hand, the party throwing the branches down would be liable to anyone who was injured while walking on the road unless a warning had been shouted.

In other cases, liability was imposed because of a failure to meet some expected standard of behaviour. Thus, a doctor would be liable for the death of a slave in his care if that care was inadequate. Lack of skill or ability was for these purposes counted as fault.

Conduct was not considered wrongful if it was done with justification. Thus, where a robber was killed in self-defence, there would be no liability unless escape had been possible.

Causation

A person was liable for his wrongful acts only if they could be said to be the cause of the loss suffered. In the earlier law, only direct physical injuries were actionable on this basis. Thus, if I directly struck your horse with a weapon, I would be liable for the resulting injury. If, however, I merely frightened your horse into stampeding off a cliff, I would not be liable. This was expressed by saying that the injury had to be *corpore corpori* (by the body, to the body). By "to the body" is meant the body of the property which was damaged, including inanimate property.

However, this requirement was gradually abandoned. The main vehicle for this development was the willingness of the praetor to allow an action *in factum* where justice demanded it. For example, if A struck B, causing B to fall on and kill C, A would be liable on an action *in factum* for C's death even though there was no direct injury. Again, where an abortifacient was supplied to a pregnant woman who died as a result of taking it, the supplier would be liable on an action *in factum*.

As with the modern law of delict, a "thin skull" rule was applied. One had to take one's victim as one found him. What this meant was that it was no defence, for example, that a slave had had a latent weakness causing him to die of an injury that would not have killed a healthy person.

PRAETORIAN DELICTS

By praetorian development, certain other delicts were recognised, although not covered in the Institutional Scheme.

For example, "*metus*" was the term used for the situation in which a person, subject to threats, was compelled to act in a way to his detriment. Fourfold damages were payable for this, although the wrongdoer could avoid liability by restoring property acquired from the victim in this manner.

"*Dolus*" meant fraud or deceit to the detriment of another. Damages for the loss suffered, or restitution of any benefit taken due to the fraud, was the appropriate remedy.

Another example was the corruption of slaves. This action lay when a person had intentionally caused the physical, mental or moral degradation of a slave. An example might be encouraging a slave to steal from his master. Liability under this action was for double damages, based on the reduction in value of the slave on account of the degradation, and also any loss caused by the slave's actions on account of the corruption. Thus, if the slave was induced to steal from the master, the value of the property stolen would be included in the measure of the damages payable.

Essential Facts

- Roman law did not have a general law of delict. Instead, specific delicts were recognised.
- Theft involved the unauthorised handling of goods with fraudulent intention. Double damages were payable, except in the case of "manifest theft", where quadruple damages were payable. Robbery differed from theft in involving violence, and gave rise to quadruple damages.
- *Iniuria* was constituted by intentional insults of many different types. No damages were payable if the insult was unintentional, or justified, or the victim was not upset by the insult.

- The first and third sections of the *lex Aquilia* imposed liability for loss caused by wrongful acts. There were thus three requirements for liability: that one party has suffered loss; that this loss was caused by the other party; and that the act causing the loss was wrongful.

- The measure of damages in an action under the *lex Aquilia* depended on which section applied. The first section applied to killing of slaves and livestock, and based the damages payable on the highest value the property had had in the year preceding the injury. The third section applied to other instances of damage to property, and damages were based on "whatever the damage shall prove to be worth in the next 30 days". The precise meaning of this is unclear.

Essential cases

Martin v McGuiness (2003): the pursuer sought damages from the defender for injuries resulting from a road accident. In preparation for the court proceedings, the defender engaged a private detective to carry out surveillance of the pursuer, to determine whether his injuries were of the extent claimed. The pursuer argued that the invasion of privacy resulting from this was actionable as *iniuria*. The court accepted that such actions might constitute *iniuria*.

Stevens v Yorkhill NHS Trust (2006): the pursuer sought damages for the removal of her daughter's brain, without the pursuer's consent, during a post-mortem examination. The court held that the unauthorised removal and retention of organs constituted *iniuria*.

Stewart's Exrx v The London, Midland & Scottish Railway Co (1943): this was an action for the death of Miss Stewart in a railway accident. In the House of Lords, Lord MacMillan discussed *iniuria* and the *lex Aquilia* and their relationship to actions for personal injury. He also commented on the role of Roman law in the development of Scots law more generally.

9 THE LAW OF THINGS: OTHER OBLIGATIONS

It will be remembered that Justinian gave a fourfold classification of obligations, into obligations arising "from a contract, as though from a contract, from a wrong, or as though from a wrong". We have already looked at obligations arising from contracts and wrongs (delicts). In this chapter, we look at those obligations arising under other heads.

OBLIGATIONS AS THOUGH FROM A CONTRACT (*QUASI EX CONTRACTU*)

The obligations arising as though from a contract form a category where the obligations arises without agreement between the parties, but in a case where nonetheless the basis of the obligation is seen as being closer to contract than to delict.

Justinian considers various types of obligation as falling under this head. This chapter looks at two of these: *negotiorum gestio* and the *conditio indebiti*, which falls under the more general heading of unjustified enrichment.

Negotiorum gestio

Negotiorum gestio is concerned with the situation where a person (the *negotiorum gestor*), interferes in the affairs of another (the principal), without the latter's consent. An example might be where the *negotiorum gestor* instructs or carries out necessary repairs to a neighbour's property. As long as the *negotiorum gestor* did not intend to act gratuitously, and provided that the other requirements for *negotiorum gestio* are met, he will be entitled to be compensated for his expenses. This is the case even though the acts of the *negotiorum gestor* are carried out without the knowledge or authorisation of the principal.

Liability to a *negotiorum gestor* will arise only where the principal is unable to act personally. For example, the principal might be absent or insane. The assumption is that he would have acted had he been able to. It is necessary, though, for the interference to be reasonable, for example where the situation is an emergency. If the matter could quite happily have waited for the principal's return, however, there will be no liability to the *gestor*. Indeed, the *gestor* himself may be liable for interfering with the principal's property if it is subsequently decided that the interference was not reasonable. Even if the interference is reasonable, the *negotiorum gestor* will be liable to the highest standard of care for any loss caused to the principal by the fault of the *gestor*.

In addition to the requirement that it be reasonable to interfere, the interference must also be objectively useful to the principal. Usefulness is, however, measured at the time of the interference. The *negotiorum gestor* will still be entitled to compensation if the benefit to the principal has been superseded. An example might be the case of accidental destruction of property after it has been repaired by the *negotiorum gestor* in circumstances where it was reasonable for him to interfere. The *negotiorum gestor* would be entitled to the usual compensation despite the subsequent destruction of the property.

Unjustified enrichment

How does the law respond to the situation in which a person receives a benefit to which he is not entitled? In the modern law, that person will be said to be unjustly enriched, and will be compelled to restore the enrichment. The purpose of the law of unjustified enrichment can broadly be said to be to rectify injustices caused by the application of the law of property. Property law, as we have seen, tends to take an objective approach to parties' rights – properly so, as a real right binds everyone. Hence, for example, the need for an act of delivery in the transfer of ownership. If third parties are to be bound by a person's real right in property, it seems only fair that it should not be possible to create or transfer the real right in secret, by intention alone. However, there remains the possibility that there is some unfairness in the parties' relationship. Suppose, for example, that by fraudulent means A induces B to transfer ownership to him. One option open to a legal system in this situation is to deny ownership to A. However, that would mean that B could recover the property even from a third party acquiring it from A with no knowledge of the fraud. An alternative is to give A ownership (a real right) but to give B a claim against A in unjustified enrichment (a personal right). This means that B has a remedy but anyone acquiring ownership in good faith from A is not affected by the fraud.

Roman law took the latter approach. However, there was no general ground of unjustified enrichment. Instead, various distinct grounds of enrichment were developed, called *condictiones*. The term "*condictio*" itself is derived from the earlier system of procedure, the *legis actiones* (see Chapter 10). In that system of procedure, the *legis actio per condictionem* gave notice to the other party of what was being claimed. The *condictio*, however, did not state the basis of the claim. It merely alleged that a particular thing or a particular sum of money was owed. The model was carried over to the later formulary procedure and, because it did not state the basis of the claim, it was found to be capable of use in a wide variety of situations, both contractual and delictual. One such situation was the contract of *mutuum* which we saw in Chapter 7. It will be remembered that, in this contract, the delivery of a thing gave rise to an obligation to restore its equivalent. In *mutuum*, the intention was to make a loan. The view developed, though, that delivery of a thing in the belief that it was due was an analogous situation, and similarly gave rise to an obligation to restore its equivalent. Gaius considers the two situations together, even though he admits that in the latter case the party who delivers the thing "intends to extinguish an obligation rather than to contract one" (G.3.91).

The situation outlined here, the claim for return of money or property transferred in the erroneous belief that it was due, took in the Justinianic law the name *"condictio indebiti"*. Various other grounds of unjustified enrichment were recognised. For example, the *condictio causa data causa non secuta* allowed recovery of money or property given in anticipation of an event that did not come to pass. An example might be an engagement ring. If the marriage did not come to pass, an obligation to return the ring arose. The *condictio ob turpem vel iniustam causam* allowed recovery where the money or property had been given for an immoral purpose, though only where the parties were not equal in immorality. Thus, money paid to a kidnapper as a ransom could be recovered, but money paid to a prostitute for her services could not. The right of a good faith possessor to be compensated for improvements to property (see Chapter 4) and the right to compensation arising when ownership is lost due to the operation of *specificatio* (see Chapter 5) could also be considered under the heading of unjustified enrichment.

OBLIGATIONS AS THOUGH FROM DELICT (*QUASI EX DELICTO*)

The cases of obligations arising as though from delict comprise a distinct group in the Institutional Scheme, set apart from other obligations. What is the basis for this classification? Various unifying factors have been suggested, such as strict or vicarious liability, or liability arising from holding some special status, but none is stated by Gaius or Justinian beyond stating that these do not fit into delict but are closer to delict than to contract.

The judge who makes the case his own

In the formulary system of procedure, there was no system of appeals against the decision of a judge. Such a judge was more in the manner of a private arbiter than a judge in the modern sense. This, of course, gave rise to risks concerning the quality of judgments for, although the non-legally qualified judge would typically take advice on legal points, there was no requirement for him to do so. On top of this, there was the risk of corruption. For this reason, the law made the "judge who makes the case his own" liable to the offended party. The party who lost out because of the judge's shortcomings could raise a new action against the judge, with the possibility of penal damages.

It is not clear what types of fault would give rise to liability on this ground. Justinian suggests that the judge was liable for any errors "even if only from ignorance" (J.4.5pr), which would suggest that the judge was liable for any error at all, making this a delict of strict liability (ie one imposing liability without fault needing to be shown). However, it would appear that liability here was based on lack of skill or judgment, which we saw in Chapter 8 was held to constitute fault. This was not, therefore, an example of strict liability.

Things thrown, poured or hanging

Any person was liable for any loss caused if someone threw or poured something from his premises, whether he was the owner or some other class of occupier. There was no need to show fault on the part of the occupier. It was enough that it was from his premises that the thing was thrown or poured.

There was also a penalty for things placed or hanging "where people come and go, which might do harm if they fell" (J.4.5.1). This was an *actio popularis*, that is to say it could be brought by any person, even if they had not suffered injury. Indeed, it need not be the case that anyone had been injured. Damages were payable for any injuries caused by the thing falling, these being a fixed sum for the death of a free man. The person liable was anyone who was responsible for placing the thing.

Shipowners, innkeepers and stablekeepers

Anyone in charge of a ship, inn or stable was liable for any theft committed there by someone in his service. There was no need to show personal fault. Innkeepers were also liable for theft or damage by permanent guests.

Essential Facts

- In addition to contracts and delicts, Justinian distinguished two further categories of obligation: obligations arising as though from contract and those arising as though from delict. These are obligations thought not to be either contractual or delictual but they were classified accordingly as they were thought to be closer to contracts or delicts.

- *Negotiorum gestio* imposes a quasi-contractual obligation when one person acts beneficially on another's behalf, but without consent. The obligation arises only when it was reasonable to carry out the act in question.

- "Unjustified enrichment" is the modern term for a number of quasi-contractual situations. Unjustified enrichment is based on the idea that, where a person has received a benefit without a proper legal basis, he should be obliged to return it. Thus, the *condictio indebiti* is a claim for the return of money or property transferred in the mistaken belief that it was due.

- Quasi-delict covers several different types of obligation arising in cases of wrongful conduct thought not to fall within the law of delicts. The basis of the classification is not clear, however. Other than the imposition of liability on "the judge who makes the case his own", the other quasi-delicts are concerned with occupiers of property. They impose strict liability for damage caused by things thrown, poured or left hanging in a public place, and on shipowners, innkeepers and stablekeepers for theft from their premises.

Essential Cases

Kolbin & Sons v Kinnear & Co (1930): during the Russian Revolution, the defenders had warehoused in Archangel goods that belonged to the pursuers. To prevent the goods falling into Bolshevist hands, the defenders shipped the goods out of the country. They then delivered the goods to a third party with no entitlement to them, without making adequate provision to protect the pursuers' interests. The third party then sold the goods, and became bankrupt while the proceeds of the sale were in his hands. The court held that the defenders were liable as *negotiorum gestores* for failure to take sufficient care of the goods.

Morgan Guaranty Trust Co of New York v Lothian Regional Council (1995): this case concerned the *condictio indebiti*. The court held that one who had made payments under an error of law was entitled to their return.

Shilliday v Smith (1998): this case concerned the *condictio causa data causa non secuta*. The parties, who were engaged, cohabited in a house owned by the defender, in anticipation of their marriage. When the relationship broke down, the pursuer sought recompense for expense she had incurred in repairs to the house. The court held that she was entitled to recompense.

McDyer v Celtic Football and Athletic Co Ltd (2000): the pursuer was injured by an item falling from the roof while attending an event at the defenders' stadium. After discussion of the sources, his argument that the quasi-delictual actions on things thrown or hanging applied was rejected, on the basis that those actions applied only to those injured while outside the building.

Drake v Dow (2006): while the pursuer was staying in the defender's bed and breakfast establishment, his computer was stolen from his room. It was not disputed that the Roman quasi-delict on innkeeper's liability had been received into Scots law. However, it was held that B&Bs were not "inns" for these purposes.

10   THE LAW OF ACTIONS

It was explained in Chapter 2 that Roman law starts off expressed in terms of actions. Early law is merely a list of remedies for particular situations. The Institutional Scheme, however, involves the separation of the substantive rights given by the law from the procedures for their enforcement, and their classification as pertaining either to the law of persons or to the law of things. What is contained in the "law of actions" in the Institutional Scheme, therefore, is the law of court procedure.

As might be expected, the procedures used in Roman litigation changed over time. Three different forms of procedure existed. The earliest was the *legis actiones* procedure. This was replaced during the Republic by the formulary procedure, which was itself superseded in the Empire by the *cognitio* procedure.

THE *LEGIS ACTIONES* PROCEDURE

The *legis actiones* (actions in law) procedure was the original form of procedure in Roman law. It had three stages, namely an oral summons, a preliminary hearing before a magistrate and a full trial before a judge.

It is a notable feature of Roman litigation at this time that the state was seen as having little role in the process. As we shall see, litigation was seen essentially as a process of private arbitration.

The oral summons

When one wanted to initiate litigation, one had first to get one's opponent into court. To do this, one began with an oral summons (*in ius vocatio*). The one receiving the summons could then go to court, or alternatively could find someone to act as a *vindex*, guaranteeing that party's appearance at some later date.

Consistently, though, with the view that litigation was a private affair, it was up to the person raising the action to get his opponent to the court. In the modern law, there might be various consequences for failure to respond to a summons to court, the most common being decree being granted in favour of the pursuer by default. In the *legis actiones* procedure, however, there were no such consequences. If the party against whom the action was raised refused to co-operate, the action could not proceed in his absence. His attendance could, however, be compelled by physical force.

The preliminary hearing

The next stage was a hearing before a magistrate, who would be the urban praetor after the creation of that office in 367 BC. It was from this stage that the *legis actiones* procedure took its name, for it was here that the relevant action had to be selected. To initiate litigation, there were three actions available. The precise procedure followed would depend on which action was selected, but in each case there would be some formal process, to which the parties had to adhere strictly. Failure to comply with the appropriate procedure (for example by selecting the wrong form of action) meant that the action was lost there and then. This high degree of formality was characteristic of the *legis actiones* procedure.

The standard action was the *sacramentum*, used when no other was prescribed by statute. This action involved the parties making formal oaths, and each depositing a sum of money as a wager on the outcome of the case. The wager was 50 *asses* (the *as* being a Roman coin), or 500 *asses* if the subject-matter of the litigation was worth more than 1,000 *asses*. The winner had his money returned, but the loser forfeited his to the State. What happened next depended on whether the action was *in rem* or *in personam* (ie whether it concerned a real right or a personal right – see Chapter 4). Where the action was *in rem*, the property concerned was brought to court. In the case of land, a symbol in the form of earth would be brought. The parties then each made formal claims to the property and then touched it with a ceremonial rod to symbolise their claim. A decision would also have to be taken on the matter of who was to have possession of the property in the interim. As we saw in Chapter 4, this would usually be the party presently in possession. In the case of an action *in personam*, however, there was no property being claimed, and so this part could be omitted. In either case, the completion of the hearing before the praetor was followed by a 30-day period before the appointment of a judge to hear the merits of the case. The purpose of the 30-day delay was to give the parties an opportunity to settle the matter out of court, which no doubt was a common outcome then as today.

Another *legis actio*, the *postulatio*, was introduced as an alternative to the *sacramentum* for certain types of action *in personam*. It was less formal, involving no wagers or formal oaths. The judge could be appointed immediately, so there was no need to wait 30 days before the next stage in the litigation could begin.

The third *legis actio*, the *condictio*, was also less formal. It was introduced in the 3rd century BC for claims for the recovery of a specific thing or sum of money. This is the action that, as we saw in Chapter 9, formed the basis for the development of the law of unjustified enrichment. However, it was not originally restricted to cases of that type. Where the action was raised under the *condictio* procedure, there was again a 30-day delay before the appointment of the judge. The *condictio* also in effect required the parties to stake an additional third of the value of the case on its outcome. Thus, in addition to being awarded the subject-matter of the case, the winner was entitled to a third of its value over and above the thing itself. Suppose, for example, that A raised an action against B for payment of 1,500 *asses*. If A won, B would be required to pay 1,500 plus an additional third, ie 2,000 *asses*. However, if A lost, he would be required to pay B a third of the value of the original claim, ie 500 *asses*. This had the effect of limiting vexatious litigation but it must also have proved a barrier to the raising of actions by those of limited means.

With all three of these *legis actiones*, the completion of the stage before the praetor, when the form of the action had been decided, was known as *litis contestatio*. At this point, the claim of the party raising the action was consumed, meaning that no further action could be raised on the same facts.

The hearing before the judge

In the preliminary hearing, the form of the action was settled. The praetor would not, however, involve himself with the merits of the case. The next stage was a full hearing, where the case would be decided on its merits. This hearing usually took place before a single judge (*iudex*). However, in some types of case the law required that the matter be considered by a panel.

Whereas the hearing before the praetor was marked by considerable formality, this stage of litigation went to the opposite extreme. There were very few rules governing the conduct of this hearing and, in accordance with the view that litigation was a private matter, little effort was made to regulate proceedings. Nor was there any scope for an appeal against the judge's decision, that decision being final. The judge was chosen by the parties, a judge being imposed on the parties by the praetor only if they could not agree.

The conduct of the hearing was a matter for the judge's discretion. However, the usual procedure was for the parties' advocates each to make speeches in support of his client's case. Oral testimony would also be taken from witnesses.

At the end of this, the judge would issue his decision, usually having taken advice from jurists if a difficult legal point had been raised. It was noted in Chapter 2 that the advocates acting in court cases were not usually experts in the law. The jurists mostly restricted themselves to providing advice on cases rather than acting themselves. The same was the case with judges. The judge would be a man drawn from the upper levels of society, acting either out of social duty or for reasons of patronage. These factors naturally affected the way in which the hearing was conducted. Advocates freely attacked the character of the opposing party. They brought in matters with no legal relevance but that were likely to bring success by lowering the opposing party in the eyes of the judge. Striking examples of this can be seen in the career of the most famous of all advocates, the late Republican orator and politician Cicero. As an example, in 70 BC Cicero acted against Gaius Verres in an action alleging corruption in his governorship of Sicily. However, his speeches contained matter of little or no relevance to the matter at hand, such as allegations of promiscuity, effeminacy and inadequacy as a military commander. Nor did he, or other advocates, hesitate in the use of rhetorical flourish to distract attention from weak points in his case.

Execution

A decision by the court in one's favour will be of little use without some mechanism for its enforcement. After all, if a debtor had been willing and able to pay up, there would have been no need for litigation in the first place. For this reason, further procedures existed for the execution of court judgments.

If the dispute concerned property, one of the parties would, as we have seen, have been awarded interim possession. If that party won the case, there would be no difficulty: he could simply keep the property. In other cases, though, it was essential to be able to compel performance. There were two further *legis actiones* for this purpose.

For the first of these, *manus iniectio* (putting in power), the debtor had 30 days from the date of the judgment to comply with it. Failing compliance within that time, the creditor was entitled to seize the debtor and take him before the magistrate. The debtor was released only if he complied with the judgment, or managed to get a *vindex* to take his place to dispute the validity of the judgment. If neither of these things happened, the creditor could imprison the debtor for 60 days, during which he would be displayed in the marketplace for 3 consecutive days in the hope that someone would pay on his behalf. If no payment was made, the debtor could be put to death or sold into slavery abroad. This was, however, reduced by the *lex Poetelia* of 326 BC to a requirement that the debtor be enslaved by the creditor until he had worked off the debt.

The law also allowed in certain cases an alternative *legis actio*: *pignoris capio* (taking of a pledge). Instead of seizure of the debtor's person, this meant seizure of the debtor's property. The creditor was allowed to retain the property until the debtor complied with the judgment.

THE FORMULARY PROCEDURE

In the later Republic, with Rome expanding rapidly both politically and economically, the high degree of formality of the *legis actiones* was found inconvenient. This formality made it unsuited to the resolution of commercial disputes, in particular. The next stage in procedural development was, however, the work of the urban praetor's colleague, the peregrine praetor.

The peregrine praetor was responsible for litigation involving non-citizens. Rome's expansion brought many such people into Rome, often as merchants. Such people needed a convenient form of procedure for the resolution of disputes, and the *legis actiones* were not available to non-citizens anyway. The peregrine praetor accordingly developed a new type of procedure, known as the formulary procedure. This substituted for the *legis actiones* standardised written statements of claim, known as formulae. This was found to be so much of an improvement that the procedure was adopted for disputes between citizens. The use of the formulary procedure by citizens was confirmed by the *lex Aebutia*, enacted around 150 BC. It was this new procedure that allowed the praetors to develop the *ius honorarium* to supplement the civil law (see Chapter 2).

Under the formulary procedure, litigation continued to be a three-stage process.

The oral summons

As with the *legis actiones*, the formulary procedure was initiated by an oral summons, giving notice of the nature of the claim. The party against whom the action was being raised had to appear personally in order for the action to proceed, but he could avoid doing this immediately in one of two ways. This first of these was, as with the *legis actiones* procedure, finding a *vindex* to act as guarantor of appearance at a specified later date.

The alternative was a *vadimonium*, which was a binding promise to appear at a later date, providing for security for appearance and a penalty for failure to appear.

It was still for the party raising the action to bring his opponent to court. However, the praetor would now assist in this in various ways. For example, the praetor might now order the seizure of the estate of the non-appearing party. Physical compulsion to attend would now be very much the last resort. There is, therefore, a move here away from the idea of litigation as a private, voluntary procedure.

The preliminary hearing

As with the *legis actiones* procedure, the next stage was a preliminary hearing before the praetor. However, this was conducted in a different manner.

In the formulary procedure, the party raising the action would appear with a draft formula, stating the grounds of the claim, in a standardised form taken from the praetor's edict. The praetor would sometimes be persuaded to allow a new formula to deal with new facts, but this would be very much the exception.

The draft formula was worded as an instruction to the judge to try the case and issue a judgment accordingly. It began with the appointment of the judge (the *nominatio*), followed by a statement of what was being claimed (the *intentio*). In cases where the judge had a discretion as to the award he made, this would be accompanied by a *demonstratio*, outlining the facts on which the claim was based. The final clause was the *condemnatio*, directing the judge either to condemn or to absolve the party defending the action. The draft formula would then be subject to a process of negotiation. If the party defending the action wanted to raise a defence (*exceptio*), this would be inserted in the formula. The other party could, if desired, insert a response (*replicatio*) to the defence. *Litis contestatio* was reached when the formula was accepted by both parties.

A sample formula is as follows:

> "Let Titius be judge. If it appears that Numerius Negidius should pay Aulus Agerius 100 *denarii*, then, if there is no agreement between Aulus Agerius and Numerius Negidius that the sum should not be sued for, or if there has been any fraud on the part of Numerius Negidius, you, judge, condemn Numerius Negidius to Aulus Agerius for 100 *denarii*; otherwise absolve him."

This sample formula appears with others in A Borkowski and P du Plessis, *Textbook on Roman Law* (3rd edn), section 3.3.2.3. "Titius" is the stock name for the judge. "Aulus Agerius" and "Numerius Negidius" are the stock names for, respectively, the party pursuing and the party defending the action. The names are puns on the verbs *agere* (to pursue (an action)), and *negare* (to deny). In a real formula, the actual parties' names would be substituted. A *denarius* is a type of Roman coin.

It can be seen in this example that Aulus Agerius is suing for payment of a specific sum of money. The part beginning "If it appears" is the *intentio*. The judge has no discretion as to what to award here: he either awards 100 *denarii* or he awards nothing. Accordingly, there is no *demonstratio*. The part beginning "you, judge" is the *condemnatio*.

It can also be seen here that the draft formula has been amended by the addition of an *exceptio* and a *replicatio*. Numerius is defending the action by admitting the debt existed, but arguing that there was an agreement between the parties that the debt would not be sued for. Aulus is responding by admitting this agreement, but alleging that Numerius obtained it by fraud.

Sometimes matters could be resolved at this stage. In some cases, the praetor could issue an interdict dealing with an interim matter, in much the same way as with an interim interdict in modern Scots law. The term "interdict" in modern law, however, has a narrower meaning, relating only to prohibitions on some action. The Roman interdicts could also require some action of the party to whom they were addressed. A prominent example was the possessory interdicts, whereby, as we have seen, the praetor awarded interim possession of property. If possession was awarded to the party raising the action, there might be no need for any further procedure. Otherwise, the matter would proceed to a hearing before a judge.

The hearing before the judge

Under the formulary procedure, the hearing before the judge proceeded in much the same way as it had under the *legis actiones* procedure, with few rules of evidence or procedure. At the end of the hearing, the judge would issue his judgment, which was subject to no appeal, although, as we saw in Chapter 9, a judge who acted improperly might be subject to quasi-delictual liability.

Execution

The methods for enforcement of judgments that had been used under the *legis actiones* procedure were not abolished with the advent of the formulary procedure. However, additional methods of enforcement were introduced.

As before, the debtor had 30 days to satisfy the judgment. If this was not done, the creditor had then to raise a new action, on the judgment, known as an *actio iudicati*.

Bonorum venditio (sale of goods) was introduced in the late Republic. The praetor would allow the creditor to seize the debtor's property. Unlike the older *pignoris capio*, this process ended in the sale of the property at auction. To discourage insolvency, the procedure also resulted in *infamia* (a form of legal disgrace, with various consequences) and the debtor remained liable for any part of the debt not satisfied by the auction.

An alternative to this was *cessio bonorum* (surrender of goods), which did not result in *infamia*. As the name suggests, this process was initiated voluntarily by the debtor. However, this was only allowed at the praetor's discretion, and only where the praetor could be satisfied that the debtor had genuine assets and that the debtor's inability to comply with the judgment was the result of misfortune.

THE *COGNITIO* PROCEDURE

In the Republic, during which these procedures developed, power was dispersed widely. However, we saw in Chapters 1 and 2 that, during the Empire, power increasingly became concentrated in the hands of the emperor and of officials answerable to him. It was inconsistent with this for judges to be exercising authority outside the control of the emperor.

The formulary system did continue into the empire. However, increasingly, the State took a direct interest in the administration of justice. It became common from the reign of Augustus onwards for magistrates to be given the task of dealing with whole cases themselves, including the hearing of evidence and the issuing of judgment. For example, Augustus gave to the consuls the role of enforcing *fideicommissa* (see Chapter 6). Later emperors followed suit in other areas. This procedure was known as a *cognitio* (investigation) because the magistrate was to investigate the facts of the case as well as settling what the legal issues were. Because this was outside the normal procedure, such an investigation was called a *cognitio extraordinaria*, a name it kept even though it in fact became the usual procedure well before the abolition of the formulary procedure in AD 342.

The summons

In the *cognitio* procedure, the summons was now a written statement of claim, delivered by a court official. Getting the party against whom the action had been raised to come to court was now a matter for public officials rather than the party raising the action.

The hearing

Instead of having two hearings, one before a magistrate and one before a judge, there was now only a single hearing. The hearing was wholly under the control of the magistrate, an inquisitorial approach being adopted.

The increased formalisation of the process allowed for the development of appeals through a hierarchy of courts. Sometimes the emperor would hear appeals and, even when this was not the case, magistrates would often request guidance on the law to apply in a particular case. As we saw in Chapter 2, the emperors' responses to such requests were an important source of law in the Empire.

Execution

Enforcement of judgments was also now in the hands of State officials. This usually involved the seizure of the debtor's property for sale at auction.

Essential Facts

- In early law, litigation was seen as essentially a private arbitration process. Litigation involved three stages, only the second of which involved a State official: the praetor. At this stage, the legal issues to be decided were settled using one of three very formal types of claim, known as *legis actiones*. The first stage was an oral summons, and the third stage was a hearing before a judge.
- Enforcement of judgments under the *legis actiones* procedure could involve the death or enslavement of the debtor, reduced in the 4th century BC to enslavement until the debt had been worked off.
- Later in the Republic, a new procedure was adopted: the formulary procedure. The main difference was at the second stage: the hearing before the praetor. Instead of using the formalistic *legis actiones*,

greater flexibility was allowed by the identification of the issues in standardised written pleadings known as formulas.

- Enforcement of judgments in the formulary system usually meant the seizure of the debtor's property for auction.
- In the Empire, the formulary system was increasingly superseded by the *cognitio* procedure. In the *cognitio* procedure, the whole process was under the control of a magistrate, with only a single hearing, in contrast with the earlier view of litigation as a form of private arbitration.

Essential Cases

Gibbs v Ruxton (2000): an accused objected to the validity of criminal proceedings on the basis that the temporary sheriff had not been validly appointed. An argument (described by the Lord Justice-General as a "welcome balm" following hours of consideration of a modern statute) was put forward–based on a text by the jurist Ulpian (D.1.14.3) on the validity of the acts of a runaway slave appointed as praetor. The argument was that, even if invalidly appointed, the acts of the temporary sheriff should be treated as valid as being acts of a *de facto* judge.

Shields v Donnelly (2000): an accused objected to criminal proceedings being moved outside the jurisdiction in which the offence was allegedly committed, arguing that this was incompetent. This argument was accepted. Two Roman texts (Modestinus, D.48.14.1 pr; and Paul, D.2.1.20), cited by Erskine, were discussed in relation to this argument.

11 THE RECEPTION OF ROMAN LAW

Most of the world's legal systems fall into one of two families. Some, largely those of countries formerly part of the British Empire, are based on English law. Examples include (most of) the United States, (most of) Canada, Australia, New Zealand and so forth. These are known as the "Common Law" jurisdictions (not to be confused with the term "common law", meaning non-statute law). Although the Common Law has received some influence from Roman law, it is largely the result of independent development by medieval English lawyers. Medieval England was in many ways precocious in its development, and the early emergence of a sophisticated court system and legal profession insulated English law from developments elsewhere. Legal education in medieval England took place in the Inns of Court and not, as it did elsewhere, in the universities.

The other major family of legal systems is the "Civil Law" family, made up of systems based on Roman law. Broadly speaking, this family is made up of the Continental jurisdictions (including some, such as Germany, covering areas that did not form part of the Roman Empire) and their former colonies, such as the countries of South America.

There is also an intermediate group of legal systems, called the "mixed systems", containing elements of both. Typically, these have received Roman law but then have come under Common Law influence. Thus, of this group, South Africa and Sri Lanka were both Dutch possessions before becoming part of the British Empire. Likewise, Louisiana was a French, then Spanish, colony before becoming one of the United States. Quebec was a French colony before becoming part of the British Empire. Scotland also falls into this group, having received Roman law before coming under English influence following the Union of 1707.

It will be seen that those countries that received Roman law during the medieval period were not necessarily those that formed part of the Roman Empire. In this chapter we explore this later history of Roman law, with particular focus on Scotland.

GLOSSATORS

For the most part, direct knowledge of Roman sources disappeared from western Europe following the fall of the Western Empire. There was naturally some survival, for conquerors usually left intact the laws of the peoples they conquered. Thus, those left behind by the retreat of Rome from the west continued to be governed by a form of Roman law. Of the Justinianic sources, parts of the *Codex* and the *Novels* were still in use, and the *Institutes* continued to be known. The survival of Justinianic works was, however, often in the form of later summaries or with later modifications. There was thus some continuity in legal practice following the fall of the Western Empire. However, the largest part of the *Corpus Iuris Civilis*, the *Digest*, was not known.

There was certainly teaching of law, and teaching of Roman law, during this period. But such work is overshadowed by the emergence of a movement of scholars collectively known as "Glossators". The Glossators, beginning with Irnerius, a grammarian at Bologna in the 11th century, began to study the Roman texts. This was part of a general renaissance in culture and commerce as Europe emerged from the Dark Ages. Urbanisation and developments in trade demanded greater legal sophistication in response, for which the written Roman law was a natural candidate. The stimulus for this development must have been the search for legal authorities for use in practice. It may be said, though, that the story that Irnerius turned to the study of Roman law in search of material for his researches as a grammarian suggests that his interests were academic rather than practical. This is not to say, however, that the Glossators were wholly uninterested in practical matters. Irnerius himself is known to have acted in a judicial capacity.

In any case, what made this revival possible was the rediscovery of the full text of the *Digest* in the late 11th century. The Glossators were teachers, presenting the Roman materials to their students. They developed understanding of the Roman texts by dealing with each text in turn, explaining doubtful points and by making comparisons with other texts. From this approach to teaching there developed their characteristic form of writing.

The Glossators produced various forms of literature. However, their characteristic approach was the addition to the text of marginal "glosses" (from which the Glossators take their name). The purpose of these glosses was to explain difficult points and cross-refer to other texts dealing with similar subject-matter. They believed Justinian's claim that no contradictions were to be found in the texts, and devoted much energy to explaining apparent contradictions. Roman sources were also updated and adapted to meet contemporary needs. Thus, what emerges from the Glossators' hands is not the law as understood in Justinian's day, and still less the classical Roman law.

The culmination of the Glossators' work was the Accursian Gloss, or *Glossa Ordinaria* (Standard Gloss), compiled by Accursius in the mid-13th century. This was a compilation of almost 97,000 glosses on the texts of the *Corpus Iuris Civilis*. It was quickly accepted as the standard commentary on the Roman texts, both for the practice of the law and as a basis for further development. It did, though, represent the limit to which the Glossators' approach could fruitfully be taken.

COMMENTATORS

The Glossators laid the foundation for study of the Roman legal texts. The development was continued by a new school called the Commentators, emerging in the 14th century, who continued the development of the Roman texts for the needs of practice. Like the Glossators, the Commentators were teachers, and much of their literature that comes down to us is in the form of lecture notes.

The Commentators' characteristic form of literature was the larger-scale commentary on the Roman texts, beyond the scale of the gloss. However, the individual texts had now been mastered, and so the Commentators were also able to develop the discussion of specific areas of law independently from the arrangement of the texts in the Roman sources. In addition to commentaries, therefore, the Commentators also produced numerous monographs on specific legal topics. The other substantial form of literature produced by the Commentators was the collection of *consilia*, or legal opinions. This attention to the needs of practice led to the Commentators interpreting the Roman texts freely, to meet these needs. They also had to account for contemporary developments in the law, such as local legislation, and not simply apply the Roman law. Nonetheless, the Roman law was always there as a subsidiary source, to supplement and fill in the gaps in the contemporary law. This process of blending Roman, feudal and canon law was important in the development of the *ius commune*.

The two most important of the Commentators were Bartolus (1314–57) and his pupil Baldus de Ubaldis. Baldus was the author of a large number of *consilia*, of which around 2,500 survive. These opinions take in the whole range of the law, including not only the Roman texts but also canon law and feudal law.

Bartolus was the author of a very large commentary on the whole of the *Corpus Iuris Civilis*. This was the major work of the period, continuing to be used into the early modern period. This was often to the extent of overshadowing other writers, and it was said that *nemo iurista nisi Bartolista* ("no one is a jurist except a Bartolist").

CANON LAW

In the medieval period, the Roman Catholic Church courts had jurisdiction, independently of the secular authorities, over a variety of areas of law, such as marriage and wills. The basis of canon law consisted of the canons of the Church, that is to say the rules laid down by the authorities of the Church, and scripture and the works of the Fathers of the Church. Although there were variations in practice in the extent to which canon law applied over local law, in principle canon law was an international system, with the secular authorities having no jurisdiction over the matters dealt with by it. Throughout western Christendom, if one had a dispute over, say, the validity of a marriage, it was not to the secular courts that one went for its resolution but to the courts of the Church, presided over by the bishop of the diocese. In northern Europe, this was ended by the Protestant Reformation, which in Scotland is dated at 1560. Even then, though, canon law as it stood at the date of Reformation was the applicable law in the fields it had covered, and so it continued to be applied, albeit now under the jurisdiction of the secular authorities.

The classical period of canon law begins with the *Decretum Gratiani*, an unofficial collection of canons made around 1140 by Gratian, a monk at Bologna. Although itself unofficial, this collection attracted study, with similar methods to those of the Glossators. As we have seen, the study of Roman law was being developed at Bologna and elsewhere at this time.

The importance of canon law for present purposes lies in its use of Roman law as a subsidiary source where this did not conflict with Church teachings. As an example, the Roman view that marriage was constituted by the parties' consent was adopted (see Chapter 3). However, the Roman position that marriage could be dissolved by the will of either party conflicted with scripture, and was not adopted.

Even when Roman rules were used, they were adapted to fit the Church's requirements. For example, it will be remembered from Chapter 3 that the Roman position on marriage was that "agreement, not sleeping together, makes a marriage" (Ulpian, D.35.1.15). This, it has been suggested, is "somewhat misleading if interpreted to mean that everything depended on the intention of the parties" (A Borkowski and P du Plessis, *Textbook on Roman Law* (3rd edn), p 127). Instead, the argument runs, consent to be married is what distinguishes marriage from other forms of cohabitation. It does not follow from this that cohabitation is not required. However, for the canonists this was used as the basis for a rule that everything did indeed depend on the intention of the parties, the sin of fornication thus being avoided where there had been consent to marriage without a marriage ceremony or cohabitation. For obvious reasons, marriage was an area in which canon law was particularly important, and it is from the principle outlined here that the Scots common law of marriage developed.

Roman influence extended beyond substantive law, for the procedure of the canon law courts was based on the Roman *cognitio* procedure (see Chapter 10). Through this medium, the Roman procedure influenced secular procedures. The Court of Session in Scotland is an example of a secular court the basis of whose procedures is so derived.

Canon law differed from Roman law in being directly applicable and in being capable of modification, through Church legislation. Nonetheless, it was said that neither Roman law nor canon law could be understood without the other. We have seen that the canon lawyers made extensive use of the Roman sources, but the process also worked the other way. It is not possible in practice to draw clear distinctions between different areas of law, and sometimes an issue of canon law would be relevant to an issue before the secular courts. For example, a person's legitimacy turned on the validity of his parents' marriage, which was a canon law matter. Illegitimacy had various consequences outside the scope of canon law, for example with succession to land, and so the secular courts would usually apply the canon law position. There were, of course, exceptions to this. A prominent example is the rejection by English law of the canon law's acceptance of legitimation by subsequent marriage, whereby a person born illegitimate is rendered legitimate if his parents subsequently marry. The consequence of this rejection would be that the same person might be considered illegitimate for matters within the jurisdiction of the secular English courts, but legitimate by the canon law courts in the same country. But, considered as a whole, canon law was an important vehicle for the reception of Roman law, applying Roman law in areas that did not otherwise experience a large-scale Reception.

THE *IUS COMMUNE*

Through the work of scholars of Roman law and through the canon law, together with the development of feudal law, there developed in Europe the phenomenon known as the *ius commune*. The term *"ius commune"* translates literally as "common law". However, it is usually left in Latin to avoid confusion with the English Common Law.

The *ius commune* was a common European legal tradition in which lawyers were educated, rather than in their native system. Roman law, above all, was used as a common legal resource. Of course, this is not to say that there was a single system of law applying throughout Europe. Local legislation was important as well. However, in an age when legal education meant Roman legal education, lawyers were bound to see the law through Romanist eyes. Even where a local rule applied, it was interpreted in Romanist terms. A Scottish example of this can be found in the Leases Act 1449, which is still in force today. In Roman law, a lease was a form of hire (see Chapter 7). As a contract, it gave only a personal right, meaning that if the landlord transferred ownership of the property to a third party the tenant's only remedy was an action against the landlord for breach of contract. He could not enforce the lease against the new owner, for only real rights were enforceable against third parties. The position was the same in the Scots common law. However, the Leases Act 1449 provided that a tenant could continue in possession notwithstanding a change in ownership. The Act nowhere uses the term "real right". But in Romanist terms, a right enforceable against a third party could be only a real right. Thus it is that, in modern Scots law, a lease is seen as a real right, with the full consequences of that designation. Those consequences go beyond those stated in the 1449 Act, and include, for example, the tenant's protection against the landlord's insolvency.

Experiences of the Reception of Roman law differed in different countries. Reception differed in pace and character in different places. The remainder of this chapter looks at some of the more significant examples of the process, which culminated in the development of national legal systems based on Roman law.

FRANCE

France was in the Middle Ages marked by a north–south divide between the *pays de droit écrit* of the south and the *pays de droit coutumier* of the north. In the former case, there had been some survival of Roman law during the Dark Ages, and so the new learning was readily received there. In the north, however, the law was based on local custom, and Roman influence was later and more gradual, although it was studied in the universities of the north.

In the 16th and early 17th centuries, Paris was the centre of the movement known as Legal Humanism, although this school of thought had adherents elsewhere. Legal Humanism was known as the *mos gallicus* (French way), as distinct from the *mos italicus* (Italian way) of the Glossators and Commentators. Humanism (which has no connection to what is nowadays called humanism) was a general historical movement, with its roots in the 15th century, marked by an interest in the critical study of history and philology. In the legal context, this meant looking critically at the ways in which the Roman texts were used. We have seen that the Glossators and Commentators took the Roman texts as they stood and freely adapted them to meet contemporary needs. The Humanists, however, criticised what they saw as a distortion of the Roman sources, which had already been distorted by Justinian. They were aware that the Justinianic texts preserved the developing law at different stages, and were interested in drawing out the historical layers of the texts in order to understand their original meaning: as with Irnerius, the first prominent Legal Humanist, Lorenzo Valla (1405–57), was brought to study of the Roman texts through the study of philology. They were interested in the relationship between law and society, seeing legal developments as reflecting changes in society. This represented a move away from the view of the law as the product of reason, to a position where the law was seen as reflective of the society that produced it.

The Humanists were very influential in the academic study of Roman law. They can be said to stand at the beginning of the discipline of jurisprudence, or legal philosophy. However, although many Humanists were prominent in legal practice, Humanist ideas had little direct influence there.

By implication, the Humanist approach challenged the idea of a *ius commune*, and was linked to the development of nationalist sentiment on the Continent. None of these developments led to the emergence of a national French legal system, however. A truly national system did not exist in France until Napoleon's *Code Civil* of 1804, based on Roman law but with modifications.

GERMANY

Germany experienced a comparatively late Reception of Roman law, from the 15th century onwards, and initially through the influence of canon law. However, when Reception did occur, it was a relatively quick process.

As elsewhere, legal fragmentation encouraged reference to experts trained in Roman law. From the point of view of two localities with differing laws, Roman law was neutral law, to which recourse could be had in disputes, and the local authorities would often adopt Roman law in any case. It was common for disputes on complex points to be resolved by seeking opinions from university law faculties. As the law faculties were staffed by Romanists, the answer would be in terms of Roman law. We see therefore Roman law being, as it were, adopted from the bottom up.

But in the Germany of the Holy Roman Empire, which saw itself as the successor to the Roman Empire, Roman law had also a political significance. Its adoption was therefore also promoted from the top down by the establishment in 1495 of the *Reichskammergericht* as a supreme court of the Holy Roman Empire, in an attempt to establish a common legal order based on Roman law.

The result of these developments was the emergence of a distinctive German approach to the Roman texts, the *Usus Modernus Pandectarum* ("Modern Usage of the *Digest*", "Pandects" being an alternative term for the *Digest*) in the 17th and early 18th centuries. Unlike the Humanists, the lawyers of this school used the Roman texts to provide practical solutions to practical legal problems, taking account also of Germanic customary law.

This development eventually culminated in codification of German law, but later than was the case in France. The codification movement was delayed till the later 19th century, although there were earlier attempts in particular parts of Germany. Part of the reason for the delay was that Germany was not unified until 1871, and so it would hardly have been practicable to impose a common code of law on it. Another reason for delay, though, was the dispute over the correct approach to take, between the "Historical School", emphasising the importance of native tradition, and the Romanists, emphasising Roman law. Work on the final Code, the *Bürgerliches Gesetzbuch* (BGB), was begun after German unification. Enacted in 1900, it combined Roman law and Germanic practice.

THE NETHERLANDS

In the Netherlands, Roman law was already in use by the 13th century, but localised customary law predominated. Encouraged by the lack of a unified legal system, though, *ius commune* influence became more pronounced in the late 15th century. In that century, two appellate courts were founded, which were staffed by Roman-trained lawyers.

Through this process, the Netherlands developed a national legal system, based on Roman law but taking into account domestic customary law. In the 17th century, the term "Roman–Dutch law" was coined by

Simon de Leeuwen for this development. The most important product of Roman–Dutch legal thinking, though, was the work of Hugo de Groot (1583–1645), better known as Grotius. Grotius made use of natural law ideas, conceived by Aquinas in the 13th century in drawing on the work of Aristotle, and further developed by later writers. He was an important figure in the development of international law, but he also contributed to domestic law in his *Introduction to the Jurisprudence of Holland*, an introductory work following the order of Justinian's *Institutes*. This book was written while Grotius was imprisoned but was published later, in 1631.

Roman–Dutch law was codified in the Dutch Civil Code (*Burgerlijk Wetboek*) in 1830, and so, as with other codified systems, resort is no longer had in practice to the Roman sources. However, uncodified Roman–Dutch law continues to be the basis of the law in former Dutch colonies, such as South Africa.

SCOTLAND

The early period

Early Scots law stood outside the general stream of these developments, and received greater influence from England than from the developing *ius commune*. The most important piece of evidence for the content of early Scots Law is a treatise, called *Regiam Majestatem* ("Royal Majesty") from its opening words, probably compiled in the early 14th century. The opening passage is adapted from that of Justinian's *Institutes*, which begins with the words *Imperatoriam Maiestatem* ("Imperial Majesty"). However, it should not be thought that this demonstrates a direct influence from Roman law. The opening, and most of the content, of *Regiam Majestatem* is lifted from an earlier English treatise called Glanvill for its author. Of course, canon law applied in Scotland as it did elsewhere. However, where canon law did not apply, non-Roman sources predominated.

An increase in Roman influence is, however, visible in the later medieval period. Scotland had no universities until the establishment of the University of St Andrews in 1413. Accordingly, for the Scot, legal education meant travel to the Continent, where legal education meant Roman legal education. Even after the foundation of the first Scottish universities, Scots continued to study abroad, particularly in France before the Reformation in 1560 and the Netherlands thereafter. Thus, when the legal profession developed in Scotland, it did so in a context where Roman law formed the foundation of legal thought. Where as in England in earlier times the professionalisation of legal practice had insulated the law from Roman influences, the converse was the case in Scotland.

In the early modern period, then, Scots law was receptive to Roman influences. When, in 1532, the Court of Session was established, it was staffed by judges trained in Roman and canon law who were, from the first, willing to resort to the *ius commune* to supplement or develop native sources.

The Institutional Writers

Modern Scots law is often considered as beginning with the Institutional Writers. The period during which the Scots Institutional Writers wrote extends from the late 17th century (Stair) to the early 19th century (Bell). It is instructive to compare these two writers for the light this consideration sheds on the manner in which English law influenced the development of Scots law after 1707.

Even a cursory look at Stair's *Institutions* shows clear Roman influence. The structure of the book is based on the Institutional Scheme of Justinian's *Institutes*. As does Justinian, Stair begins with a short section on the general principles of law. It is true that he differs from Justinian in putting marriage and the law of parent and child in with obligations, which takes up the rest of Book I. However, the rest of the book follows Justinian, down to the coverage of procedure (actions, in the terminology of Gaius and Justinian) in Book IV. As in Justinian's *Institutes*, property is next, taking in Book II and part of Book III. Again faithful to Justinian's approach, this is followed in the remainder of Book III by succession.

When we turn to matters of detail, we again see in Stair's *Institutions* clear signs of Roman influence. Stair characteristically uses Roman law sources to give the general principle applying in a particular area. Points of detail are then filled in with native sources, but always in the context of a framework fundamentally informed by Romanist legal thinking. That such a book could have been written for legal practice by an eminent judge and practitioner demonstrates the depth of the roots laid down in Scotland by Roman law.

We see the same in the Institutional Writers of the 18th century, Erskine and Bankton. However, during this century we begin to see influence from English law, particularly in commercial matters. This influence became even stronger in the 19th century. One might look at Bell's *Principles*, for example, the first edition of which was published in 1829. In the same way as Justinian's *Institutes*, this was intended as an elementary work, primarily for students. However, there is little resemblance in terms of structure. In terms of content, although extensive use is made of Roman and *ius commune* sources, substantial use is also made of English cases and textbooks. The same is true with Bell's major work, the *Commentaries*, first published in 1800 as the *Treatise on the Law of Bankruptcy in Scotland* and subsequently expanded. Unlike the earlier Scots Institutional works, this book makes no claim to be comprehensive, concentrating on commercial topics, and makes no attempt to be systematic in its structure. Like the *Principles*, the *Commentaries* also make free use of English authorities alongside native and Romanist sources.

The position today

English influence on Scots law since 1707 has been such that there has been a tendency on the part of some to downplay the influence of Roman law. Modern textbooks on the Scottish legal system often disregard Roman law as a source of law, or treat it as being of only historical interest. It is true that many areas of Scots law have been strongly influenced by English law. This is particularly true in commercial law. It is also true in areas such as delictual liability for negligence that have only become significant areas of legal practice in more recent times. Yet we have seen that there are many areas in which Scots law is identical or very similar to Roman law. Particularly in property law and the law of obligations, Roman law is the source of many of the fundamental principles of Scots law. And the importance of Roman law is not merely historical, for we have seen numerous cases where arguments have been put forward drawing directly on the Roman sources. For these reasons, the study of Roman law remains beneficial to the aspiring Scots lawyer.

Essential Facts

- Although knowledge of Roman law was only very imperfectly preserved in western Europe during the Dark Ages, the study of Roman law was revived in Bologna by Irnerius, the first of the school of Glossators, in the 11th century. This followed the rediscovery of the *Digest*. The characteristic form of literature produced by the Glossators was the marginal gloss, explaining difficult terms and cross-referencing to other texts dealing with the issue at hand.
- The culmination of the Glossators' work was the compilation by Accursius of the Accursian Gloss in the mid-13th century. This was

a large collection of glosses which became the standard reference work on the *Corpus Iuris Civilis*.

- From the 14th century, study of the Roman texts was further developed by a new school, called the Commentators. The Commentators tended to have a greater interest in the practical application of the law than did the Glossators.

- Another vehicle through which Roman law was received into medieval law was canon law. Canon law was the law of the Roman Catholic Church, which had jurisdiction over a range of matters. The Church courts used Roman law as a subsidiary source of law.

- The work of scholars of Roman law, combined with canon law and feudal law, resulted in the development of a *ius commune*, a common European legal tradition, forming the basis of the development of individual national systems of law.

- Scots law was also influenced by the *ius commune*, and Roman sources are still directly referred to today in the courts.

INDEX

NOTES

NOTES

NOTES

NOTES

NOTES

NOTES